-Country- I TALIAN *-Cooking-*

Publications International, Ltd.
Favorite Brand Name Recipes at www.fbnr.com

Illustrated by Roberta Polfus.

Pictured on the front cover: Zesty Artichoke Pesto Sauce *(page 88)*.

Pictured on the back cover *(top to bottom):* Skewered Antipasto *(page 4)*, Artichoke Frittata *(page 152)* and Poached Seafood Italiano *(page 122)*.

ISBN: 1-4127-2060-5

Library of Congress Control Number: 2004110629

Manufactured in China.

8 7 6 5 4 3 2 1

Microwave Cooking: Microwave ovens vary in wattage. Use the cooking times as guidelines and check for doneness before adding more time.

Preparation/Cooking Times: Preparation times are based on the approximate amount of time required to assemble the recipe before cooking, baking, chilling or serving. These times include preparation steps such as measuring, chopping and mixing. The fact that some preparations and cooking can be done simultaneously is taken into account. Preparation of optional ingredients and serving suggestions is not included.

Contents

Appetizers

Skewered Antipasto

Makes 12 to 14 skewers

1 jar (8 ounces) SONOMA® marinated dried tomatoes
1 pound (3 medium) new potatoes, cooked until tender
1 cup drained cooked egg tortellini and/or spinach tortellini
1 tablespoon chopped fresh chives *or* 1 teaspoon dried chives
1 tablespoon chopped fresh rosemary *or* 1 teaspoon dried rosemary
2 cups bite-sized vegetable pieces (such as celery, bell peppers, radishes, carrots, cucumber and green onions)

Drain oil from tomatoes into medium bowl. Place tomatoes in small bowl; set aside. Cut potatoes into 1-inch cubes. Add potatoes, tortellini, chives and rosemary to oil in medium bowl. Stir to coat with oil; cover and marinate 1 hour at room temperature. To assemble, alternately thread tomatoes, potatoes, tortellini and vegetables onto 6-inch skewers.

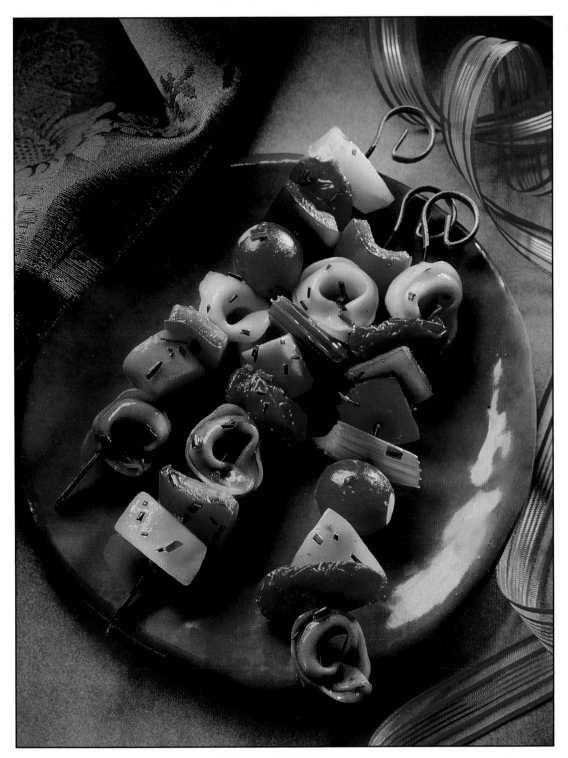

Skewered Antipasto

Artichoke Crostini
Makes 4 servings

  1 jar (6 ounces) marinated artichoke hearts, drained and chopped
  3 green onions, chopped
  5 tablespoons grated Parmesan cheese, divided
  2 tablespoons mayonnaise
12 slices French bread (½ inch thick)
    Red bell pepper for garnish (optional)

1. Preheat broiler. Combine artichokes, green onions, 3 tablespoons cheese and mayonnaise in small bowl; mix well.

2. Arrange bread slices on baking sheet. Broil 4 to 5 inches from heat source 2 to 3 minutes on each side or until lightly browned.

3. Spoon about 1 tablespoon artichoke mixture on each bread slice and sprinkle with remaining cheese. Broil 1 to 2 minutes or until cheese is melted and lightly browned. Garnish crostini with red bell pepper, if desired.

Prep and Cook Time: 25 minutes

Tip: Crostini means "little toasts" in Italian. They are traditionally small, thin slices of toasted bread that are brushed with olive oil and spread with a variety of toppings.

Artichoke Crostini

Savory Onion Focaccia

Makes 8 appetizer servings

   1 pound frozen pizza or bread dough*
   1 tablespoon olive oil
   1 clove garlic, minced
1⅓ cups *French's®* French Fried Onions, divided
   1 cup (4 ounces) shredded mozzarella cheese
   ½ pound plum tomatoes (4 small), thinly sliced
   2 teaspoons fresh chopped rosemary *or* ½ teaspoon dried rosemary
   3 tablespoons grated Parmesan cheese

Pizza dough can be found in frozen section of supermarket. Thaw in refrigerator before using.

Bring pizza dough to room temperature. Grease 15×10-inch jelly-roll pan. Roll or pat dough into rectangle same size as pan on floured board.** Transfer dough to pan.

Combine oil and garlic in small bowl; brush onto surface of dough. Cover loosely with kitchen towel. Let dough rise at room temperature 25 minutes. Prick dough with fork.

Preheat oven to 450°F. Bake dough 20 minutes or until edges and bottom of crust are golden. Sprinkle *1 cup* French Fried Onions and mozzarella cheese over dough. Arrange tomatoes over cheese; sprinkle with rosemary. Bake 5 minutes or until cheese melts.

Sprinkle with remaining ⅓ *cup* onions and Parmesan cheese. Bake 2 minutes or until onions are golden. To serve, cut into rectangles.

**If dough is too hard to roll, allow to rest on floured board.*

Prep Time: 30 minutes
Cook Time: 27 minutes

Savory Onion Focaccia

Grilled Antipasto Platter

Makes 8 appetizer servings or 4 main-dish servings

16 medium scallops
16 medium shrimp, shelled and deveined
12 mushrooms (about 1 inch diameter)
 3 ounces thinly sliced prosciutto or deli-style ham
16 slender asparagus spears
 1 jar (6½ ounces) marinated artichoke hearts, drained
 2 medium zucchini, cut lengthwise into slices
 1 large or 2 small red bell peppers, cored, seeded and cut into 1-inch-wide strips
 1 head radicchio, cut lengthwise into quarters (optional)
   Lemon Baste (recipe follows)
   Lemon wedges

Soak 12 long bamboo skewers in water for at least 20 minutes to prevent burning. Thread 4 scallops on each of 4 skewers and 4 shrimp on each of another 4 skewers. Thread 6 mushrooms on each of 2 more skewers. Cut prosciutto into 2×1-inch strips. Wrap 2 asparagus spears together with 2 strips of prosciutto; secure with toothpick. Repeat with remaining asparagus. Wrap each artichoke heart in 1 strip of prosciutto; thread on 2 remaining skewers. Place skewers, asparagus, zucchini and bell peppers on baking sheet. Reserve ¼ cup Lemon Baste. Brush remaining Lemon Baste liberally over ingredients on baking sheet.

Spread medium KINGSFORD® Briquets in wide single layer over bed of grill. Oil hot grid to help prevent sticking. Grill skewers, asparagus bundles, zucchini and red peppers, on uncovered grill, 7 to 12 minutes until vegetables are tender, seafood firms up and turns opaque and prosciutto wrapped around vegetables is crisp, turning once or twice. Remove each item from grill to large serving platter as it is done. Pour remaining baste over all. Serve hot or at room temperature. Garnish with radicchio and lemon wedges.

Lemon Baste: Whisk ½ cup olive oil, ¼ cup lemon juice, ½ teaspoon salt and ¼ teaspoon black pepper in small bowl until well blended. Makes about ¾ cup.

Grilled Antipasto Platter

Chicken Pesto Pizza

Makes about 20 squares

    1 loaf (1 pound) frozen bread dough, thawed
       Nonstick cooking spray
    8 ounces chicken tenders, cut into ½-inch pieces
    ½ red onion, cut into quarters and thinly sliced
    ¼ cup prepared pesto
    2 large plum tomatoes, seeded and diced
    1 cup (4 ounces) shredded pizza cheese blend or mozzarella cheese

1. Preheat oven to 375°F. Roll out bread dough on floured surface to 14×8-inch rectangle. Transfer to baking sheet sprinkled with cornmeal. Cover loosely with plastic wrap and let rise 20 to 30 minutes.

2. Meanwhile, spray large skillet with cooking spray; heat over medium heat. Add chicken; cook and stir 2 minutes. Add onion and pesto; cook and stir 3 to 4 minutes or until chicken is cooked through. Stir in tomatoes; remove from heat and let cool slightly.

3. Spread chicken mixture evenly over bread dough within 1 inch of edges. Sprinkle with cheese.

4. Bake on bottom rack of oven about 20 minutes or until crust is golden brown. Cut into 2-inch squares.

Chicken Pesto Pizza

Italian-Style Stuffed Mushrooms
Makes about 20 mushrooms

2 pounds large mushrooms (about 2 inches each)
½ cup (1 stick) I CAN'T BELIEVE IT'S NOT BUTTER!® Spread
⅓ cup chopped onion
1 tablespoon chopped garlic
1 cup Italian seasoned dry bread crumbs
⅔ cup shredded mozzarella cheese (about 2½ ounces)
¼ cup grated Parmesan cheese
2 tablespoons chopped fresh parsley
1 tablespoon red wine vinegar
⅛ teaspoon ground black pepper
¼ teaspoon salt

Preheat oven to 400°F.

Remove and chop mushroom stems.

In 12-inch skillet, melt I Can't Believe It's Not Butter!® Spread over medium-high heat and cook mushroom stems and onion, stirring occasionally, 5 minutes or until tender.

Add garlic and cook 30 seconds. In medium bowl, pour mushroom mixture over bread crumbs. Stir in cheeses, parsley, vinegar and pepper.

Sprinkle mushroom caps with salt. On baking sheet, arrange mushroom caps; evenly spoon mushroom mixture into mushroom caps.

Bake 25 minutes or until mushrooms are tender and golden.

Tuscan White Bean Crostini

Marinated Antipasto Kabobs

Makes 20 kabobs

½ (9-ounce) package spinach three-cheese tortellini or plain tortellini
1 package (9 ounces) frozen artichoke hearts, thawed
20 small fresh mushrooms, stems removed
1 large red bell pepper, cut into 20 equal pieces
½ cup white balsamic or white wine vinegar
¼ cup grated Parmesan cheese
¼ cup minced fresh basil
2 tablespoons Dijon mustard
1 tablespoon olive oil
½ teaspoon sugar
¼ teaspoon black pepper
20 cherry tomatoes

1. Cook tortellini according to package directions. Drain well. Cool slightly; cover and refrigerate until ready to assemble kabobs.

2. Cook artichokes according to package directions; drain. Immediately add artichokes to bowl of ice water to stop cooking process. Let stand 1 to 2 minutes; drain well. Place artichokes in large resealable plastic food storage bag. Add mushrooms and bell pepper.

3. Combine vinegar, cheese, basil, mustard, oil, sugar and black pepper in small bowl; mix well. Add to vegetable mixture in plastic bag; seal bag. Turn bag over several times to coat ingredients evenly. Refrigerate several hours or overnight, turning bag occasionally.

4. Remove vegetables from marinade, reserving marinade. Arrange vegetables on skewers alternately with tortellini and tomatoes; place on serving platter. Drizzle with reserved marinade, if desired.

Tip: Don't clean mushrooms until just before you're ready to use them (they will absorb water and become mushy). Wipe them with a damp paper towel or rinse them under cold running water and blot dry.

Marinated Antipasto Kabobs

21

Caponata
Makes approximately 4½ cups

 1 pound eggplant, cut into ½-inch cubes
 3 large cloves garlic, minced
¼ cup olive oil
 1 can (14½ ounces) DEL MONTE® Diced Tomatoes with Basil,
   Garlic & Oregano
 1 medium green pepper, finely chopped
 1 can (2¼ ounces) chopped ripe olives, drained
 2 tablespoons lemon juice
 1 teaspoon dried basil, crushed
 1 baguette French bread, cut into ¼-inch slices

1. Cook eggplant and garlic in oil in large skillet over medium heat
5 minutes. Season with salt and pepper, if desired.

2. Stir in remaining ingredients except bread. Cook, uncovered, 10 minutes
or until thickened.

3. Cover and chill. Serve with bread.

Prep Time: 10 minutes
Cook Time: 15 minutes
Chill Time: 2 hours

Tip: When purchasing eggplant, look for a firm
      eggplant that is heavy for its size, with tight,
      glossy, deeply-colored skin and bright green stem.

Stuffed Portobello Mushrooms

Makes 4 servings

4 portobello mushrooms (4 ounces each)
¼ cup olive oil
2 cloves garlic, pressed
6 ounces crumbled goat cheese
2 ounces prosciutto or thinly sliced ham, chopped
¼ cup chopped fresh basil
   Mixed salad greens

Remove stems and gently scrape gills from underside of mushrooms; discard stems and gills. Brush mushroom caps with combined oil and garlic. Combine cheese, prosciutto and basil in medium bowl. Grill mushrooms, top side up, on covered grill over medium KINGSFORD® Briquets 4 minutes. Turn mushrooms over; fill caps with cheese mixture, dividing equally. Cover and grill 3 to 4 minutes longer until cheese mixture is warm. Remove mushrooms from grill; cut into quarters. Serve on mixed greens, if desired.

Fast Pesto Focaccia

Makes 16 servings

1 can (10 ounces) pizza crust dough
2 tablespoons prepared pesto
4 sun-dried tomatoes packed in oil, drained

1. Preheat oven to 425°F. Lightly grease 8×8-inch pan. Unroll pizza dough; fold in half and pat into pan.

2. Spread pesto evenly over dough. Chop tomatoes or snip with kitchen scissors; sprinkle over pesto. Press tomatoes into dough. Make indentations in dough every 2 inches using handle of wooden spoon.

3. Bake 10 to 12 minutes or until golden brown. Cut into 16 squares; serve warm or at room temperature.

Mushroom Parmesan Crostini
Makes 12 crostini

　1 tablespoon olive oil
　1 clove garlic, finely chopped
　1 cup chopped mushrooms
　1 loaf Italian or French bread (about 12 inches long), cut into 12 slices
　　　and toasted
　¾ cup RAGÚ® Pizza Quick® Sauce
　¼ cup grated Parmesan cheese
　1 tablespoon finely chopped fresh basil leaves or 1 teaspoon dried basil leaves

Preheat oven to 375°F. In 8-inch nonstick skillet, heat olive oil over medium heat and cook garlic 30 seconds. Add mushrooms and cook, stirring occasionally, 2 minutes or until liquid evaporates.

On baking sheet, arrange bread slices. Evenly spread Ragú Pizza Quick Sauce on bread slices, then top with mushroom mixture, cheese and basil. Bake 15 minutes or until heated through.

Recipe Tip: Many varieties of mushrooms are available in supermarkets and specialty grocery stores. Shiitake, portobello and cremini mushrooms all have excellent flavor.

Mushroom Parmesan Crostini

Soups and Salads

Pasta e Fagioli

Makes 8 servings

    2 tablespoons olive oil
    1 cup chopped onion
    3 cloves garlic, minced
    2 cans (14½ ounces each) Italian-style stewed tomatoes, undrained
    3 cups reduced-sodium chicken broth
    1 can (about 15 ounces) cannellini beans (white kidney beans), undrained*
    ¼ cup chopped fresh Italian parsley
    1 teaspoon dried basil leaves
    ¼ teaspoon black pepper
    4 ounces uncooked small shell pasta

One can (about 15 ounces) Great Northern beans, undrained, can be substituted for cannellini beans.

1. Heat oil in 4-quart Dutch oven over medium heat until hot; add onion and garlic. Cook and stir 5 minutes or until onion is tender.

2. Stir tomatoes with juice, chicken broth, beans with liquid, parsley, basil and pepper into Dutch oven; bring to a boil over high heat, stirring occasionally. Reduce heat to low. Simmer, covered, 10 minutes.

3. Add pasta to Dutch oven. Simmer, covered, 10 to 12 minutes or until pasta is just tender. Serve immediately. Garnish as desired.

Pasta e Fagioli

Pepperoni Pasta Salad

Makes 8 to 10 servings

1 package (16 ounces) BARILLA® Castellane, cooked according to package
  directions
6 ounces sliced pepperoni, cut into quarters
4 ounces shredded Cheddar cheese
½ red onion, chopped
½ green pepper, chopped
1 small tomato, cubed
½ small can chopped black olives
¾ cup Italian salad dressing

1. Thoroughly rinse castellane in cold water; drain and place in large serving
bowl. Add remaining ingredients except salad dressing.

2. About 1 hour before serving, add salad dressing and toss to coat. Toss
again just before serving, adding additional salad dressing if necessary.

*Tip: The only time pasta should be rinsed after
cooking is when it will be used in a salad.
Rinsing cools the pasta and washes away
excess starch, which causes sticking.*

Pepperoni Pasta Salad

Cioppino
Makes about 14 cups

2 tablespoons olive or vegetable oil
1½ cups chopped onion
1 cup chopped celery
½ cup chopped green bell pepper
1 large clove garlic, minced
1 can (28 ounces) CONTADINA® Recipe Ready Crushed Tomatoes
1 can (6 ounces) CONTADINA® Tomato Paste
1 teaspoon Italian herb seasoning
1 teaspoon salt
½ teaspoon ground black pepper
2 cups water
1 cup dry red wine or chicken broth
3 pounds white fish, shrimp, scallops, cooked crab, cooked lobster, clams and/or oysters (in any proportion)

1. Heat oil in large saucepan. Add onion, celery, bell pepper and garlic; sauté until vegetables are tender. Add tomatoes, tomato paste, Italian seasoning, salt, black pepper, water and wine.

2. Bring to a boil. Reduce heat to low; simmer, uncovered, for 15 minutes.

3. To prepare fish and seafood: scrub clams and/or oysters under running water. Place in ½-inch boiling water in separate large saucepan; cover. Bring to a boil. Reduce heat to low; simmer just until shells open, about 3 minutes. Set aside.

4. Cut crab, lobster, fish and scallops into bite-size pieces.

5. Shell and devein shrimp. Add fish to tomato mixture; simmer 5 minutes. Add scallops and shrimp; simmer 5 minutes.

6. Add crab, lobster and reserved clams and/or oysters; simmer until heated through.

Prep Time: 30 minutes
Cook Time: 35 minutes

Cioppino

Rigatoni Salad

Makes about 8 servings

12 ounces uncooked rigatoni pasta, cooked
1 to 2 cups chopped greens, such as arugula, frisée or any crisp lettuce
1 bag (10 ounces) frozen snow peas or sugar snap peas, thawed
½ pound cherry tomatoes, cut into halves
1 medium red or yellow bell pepper, cut into thin strips
½ red onion, cut into thin strips
⅓ cup sliced black olives
⅓ to ½ cup Italian salad dressing
    Grated Parmesan cheese (optional)

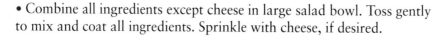

• Combine all ingredients except cheese in large salad bowl. Toss gently to mix and coat all ingredients. Sprinkle with cheese, if desired.

Note: Vary the amounts of each ingredient according to your taste. Substitute steamed green beans (whole or cut) for the peas or add steamed, sliced carrots, zucchini or yellow squash.

Tomato, Prosciutto & Fresh Mozzarella Salad

Makes 4 servings

1 package (10 ounces) DOLE® Organic Salad Blend Spring Mix with Herbs or
    Baby Lettuces Salad
1 cup yellow and red pear or cherry tomatoes, halved
1½ ounces prosciutto, chopped or 5 strips bacon, cooked, drained and crumbled
4 ounces fresh mozzarella cheese, drained and cut into bits or regular mozzarella
    cheese, cut into julienne strips
1 cup sliced red onion
1 cup croutons
¼ cup prepared balsamic vinaigrette dressing

• Combine salad blend, tomatoes, prosciutto, cheese, onion and croutons in large bowl.

• Pour vinaigrette over salad; toss to evenly coat.

Prep Time: 20 minutes

Rigatoni Salad

Fennel, Olive and Radicchio Salad
Makes 4 servings

11 Italian- or Greek-style black olives, divided
¼ cup olive oil
 1 tablespoon lemon juice
 1 flat anchovy fillet *or* ½ teaspoon anchovy paste
¼ teaspoon salt
   Generous dash black pepper
   Generous dash sugar
 1 fresh fennel bulb
 1 head radicchio*
   Fennel tops for garnish

*Radicchio, a tart red chicory, is available in large supermarkets and specialty food shops. If it is not available, 2 heads of Belgian endive can be substituted. Although it does not provide the dramatic red color, it will provide a similar texture, and its slightly bitter flavor will go well with the robust dressing and the sweet anise flavor of fennel.

1. For dressing, cut 3 olives in half; remove and discard pits. Place pitted olives, oil, lemon juice and anchovy in food processor or blender; process 5 seconds. Add salt, pepper and sugar; process until olives are finely chopped, about 5 seconds more. Set aside.

2. Cut off and discard fennel stalks. Cut off and discard root end at base of fennel bulb and any discolored parts of bulb. Cut fennel bulb lengthwise into 8 wedges; separate each wedge into segments.

3. Separate radicchio leaves; rinse thoroughly under running water. Drain well.

4. Arrange radicchio leaves, fennel and remaining olives on serving plate. Spoon dressing over salad. Garnish, if desired. Serve immediately.

Southern Italian Clam Chowder

Makes 8 cups

2 slices bacon, diced
1 cup chopped onion
½ cup chopped peeled carrots
½ cup chopped celery
2 cans (14.5 ounces each) CONTADINA® Recipe Ready Diced Tomatoes, undrained
1 can (8 ounces) CONTADINA® Tomato Sauce
1 bottle (8 ounces) clam juice
½ teaspoon chopped fresh rosemary *or* ¼ teaspoon dried rosemary leaves, crushed
⅛ teaspoon ground black pepper
2 cans (6.5 ounces each) chopped clams, undrained

1. Sauté bacon in large saucepan until crisp. Add onion, carrots and celery; sauté for 2 to 3 minutes or until vegetables are tender.

2. Stir in undrained tomatoes, tomato sauce, clam juice, rosemary and pepper. Bring to a boil.

3. Reduce heat to low; simmer, uncovered, for 15 minutes. Stir in clams and juice. Simmer for 5 minutes or until heated through.

Prep Time: 8 minutes
Cook Time: 23 minutes

Italian Bread Salad

Makes 4 servings

1 loaf (about 12 ounces) hearty peasant-style bread (such as sourdough,
    rosemary-olive oil or roasted garlic)
1 cup sliced red onion
1 teaspoon minced garlic
⅓ cup prepared balsamic and olive oil vinaigrette
1½ cups grape tomatoes or cherry tomatoes, cut into halves
⅓ cup pitted oil- or salt-cured black and green olives
1 package European salad mix or pre-washed baby spinach
    Grated Parmesan cheese
    Freshly ground black pepper to taste

1. Preheat oven to 250°F. Tear bread into large cubes, about the size of marshmallows. Place on baking sheet. Bake 10 to 15 minutes or until slightly dry but not browned. Set aside to cool.

2. Place onion slices and garlic in large salad bowl. Add vinaigrette and stir to coat. Set aside a few minutes to allow flavors to blend.

3. Add tomatoes and olives; stir gently to coat with dressing. Add greens, bread cubes and Parmesan; toss gently. Add more vinaigrette if needed and season with black pepper.

Tip: You can use day-old bread that has started to dry out for this recipe. Bread that is a little too hard or stale can be softened by sprinkling it with water. Gently squeeze the bread in your hands to remove excess moisture.

Italian Bread Salad

Quick Tuscan Bean, Tomato and Spinach Soup

Makes 4 (1½-cup) servings

2 cans (14½ ounces each) diced tomatoes with onions, undrained
1 can (14½ ounces) reduced-sodium chicken broth
2 teaspoons sugar
2 teaspoons dried basil leaves
¾ teaspoon reduced-sodium Worcestershire sauce
1 can (15 ounces) cannellini or Great Northern beans, rinsed and drained
3 ounces fresh baby spinach leaves or chopped spinach leaves, stems removed
1 tablespoon extra-virgin olive oil

1. Combine tomatoes with juice, chicken broth, sugar, basil and Worcestershire sauce in Dutch oven or large saucepan; bring to a boil over high heat. Reduce heat and simmer, uncovered, 10 minutes.

2. Stir in beans and spinach; cook 5 minutes longer or until spinach is tender.

3. Remove from heat; stir in oil just before serving.

Tip: Baby spinach is often sold already bagged and washed. Before purchasing, inspect the package closely to make sure there are no wet spots or brown edges on individual leaves, and that the leaves aren't sticking together.

Quick Tuscan Bean, Tomato and Spinach Soup

Artichoke and Olive Salad

Makes 10 servings

1 pound dry rotini pasta
2 cans (14.5 ounces each) CONTADINA® Recipe Ready Diced Tomatoes with
     Roasted Garlic, undrained
1 jar (6 ounces) artichoke hearts packed in water, drained, sliced
½ cup Italian dressing
1 can (2.25 ounces) sliced pitted ripe olives, drained
¼ cup chopped fresh parsley *or* 2 teaspoons dried parsley flakes, crushed
¼ cup sliced green onions
½ cup sliced almonds, toasted

1. Cook pasta according to package directions; drain and rinse in cold water.

2. Combine pasta, undrained tomatoes, artichoke hearts, dressing, olives, parsley and green onions in large bowl; toss well.

3. Cover. Chill before serving. Sprinkle with almonds just before serving.

Green Bean Salad

Makes 6 servings

1 pound fresh green beans, trimmed
3 tablespoons lemon juice
1 tablespoon FILIPPO BERIO® Extra Virgin Olive Oil
½ teaspoon dried oregano leaves
    Salt

In medium saucepan, cook beans in boiling salted water 10 to 15 minutes or until tender. Drain well; cool slightly. In small bowl, whisk together lemon juice, olive oil and oregano. Pour over green beans; toss until lightly coated. Cover; refrigerate several hours or overnight before serving. Season to taste with salt.

Note: Salad may also be served as an appetizer.

Hearty Tortellini Soup

Makes 4 servings

1 small red onion, chopped
2 medium carrots, chopped
2 ribs celery, thinly sliced
1 small zucchini, chopped
2 plum tomatoes, chopped
2 cloves garlic, minced
2 cans (14½ ounces each) chicken broth
1 can (15 to 19 ounces) red kidney beans, rinsed and drained
2 tablespoons *French's*® Worcestershire Sauce
1 package (9 ounces) refrigerated tortellini pasta

1. Heat *2 tablespoons oil* in 6-quart saucepot or Dutch oven over medium-high heat. Add vegetables, tomatoes and garlic. Cook and stir 5 minutes or until vegetables are crisp-tender.

2. Add broth, *½ cup water,* beans and Worcestershire. Heat to boiling. Stir in pasta. Return to boiling. Cook 5 minutes or until pasta is tender, stirring occasionally. Serve with crusty bread and grated Parmesan cheese, if desired.

Prep Time: 15 minutes
Cook Time: 10 minutes

Marinated Vegetable Salad

Makes 6 servings

3 tablespoons plus 1½ teaspoons white wine vinegar
2 tablespoons minced fresh basil *or* ½ teaspoon dried basil leaves
½ teaspoon salt
⅛ teaspoon black pepper
   Dash sugar
6 tablespoons olive oil
2 ripe medium tomatoes
⅓ cup pitted green olives
⅓ cup Italian- or Greek-style black olives
1 head leaf or red leaf lettuce
1 small head curly endive
2 heads Belgian endive

1. For dressing, place vinegar, basil, salt, pepper and sugar in blender or food processor. With motor running, add oil in slow steady stream until thoroughly blended.

2. Cut tomatoes into wedges. Combine tomatoes and green and black olives in medium bowl. Add dressing; toss lightly. Cover; let stand at room temperature 30 minutes to blend flavors, stirring occasionally.

3. Rinse leaf lettuce and curly endive; drain well. Refrigerate greens until ready to assemble salad. Core Belgian endive and separate leaves; rinse and drain well.

4. To serve, layer leaf lettuce, curly endive and Belgian endive leaves in large, shallow serving bowl.

5. Remove tomatoes and olives with slotted spoon and place on top of greens. Spoon remaining dressing over salad. Serve immediately or cover and refrigerate up to 30 minutes.

Marinated Vegetable Salad

Hearty Pasta and Chick-Pea Chowder

Makes 6 servings (about 7 cups)

6 ounces uncooked rotini pasta
2 tablespoons olive oil
¾ cup chopped onion
½ cup thinly sliced carrot
½ cup chopped celery
2 cloves garlic, minced
¼ cup all-purpose flour
1½ teaspoons dried Italian seasoning
⅛ teaspoon red pepper flakes
⅛ teaspoon black pepper
2 cans (14½ ounces each) chicken broth
1 can (19 ounces) chick-peas, rinsed and drained
1 can (14½ ounces) Italian-style stewed tomatoes, undrained
6 slices bacon
Grated Parmesan cheese

1. Cook rotini according to package directions. Rinse, drain and set aside.

2. Meanwhile, heat oil in 4-quart Dutch oven over medium-high heat until hot. Add onion, carrot, celery and garlic. Cook and stir over medium heat 5 to 6 minutes or until vegetables are crisp-tender.

3. Remove from heat. Stir in flour, Italian seasoning, red pepper flakes and black pepper until well blended. Gradually stir in broth. Return to heat and bring to a boil, stirring frequently. Boil, stirring constantly, 1 minute. Reduce heat to medium. Stir in cooked pasta, chick-peas and tomatoes. Cook 5 minutes or until heated through.

4. Meanwhile, place bacon between double layer of paper towels on paper plate. Microwave at HIGH 5 to 6 minutes or until bacon is crisp. Drain and crumble.

5. Sprinkle each serving with bacon and grated cheese. Serve immediately.

Hearty Pasta and Chick-Pea Chowder

Primavera Tortellini en Brodo

Makes 2 servings

2 cans (14½ ounces each) reduced-sodium chicken broth
1 package (9 ounces) refrigerated fresh tortellini (cheese, chicken or sausage)
2 cups frozen mixed vegetables, such as broccoli, green beans, onions and red
　　bell peppers
1 teaspoon dried basil leaves
　Dash hot pepper sauce
2 teaspoons cornstarch
1 tablespoon water
¼ cup grated Romano or Parmesan cheese

1. Pour broth into large deep skillet. Cover and bring to a boil over high heat. Add tortellini; reduce heat to medium-high. Cook, uncovered, until pasta is tender, stirring occasionally. (Check package directions for approximate timing.)

2. Transfer tortellini to medium bowl with slotted spoon; keep warm.

3. Add vegetables, basil and hot pepper sauce to broth; bring to a boil. Reduce heat to medium; simmer about 3 minutes or until vegetables are crisp-tender.

4. Blend cornstarch and water in small cup until smooth. Stir into broth mixture. Cook about 2 minutes or until liquid thickens slightly, stirring frequently. Return tortellini to skillet; heat through. Ladle into shallow soup bowls; sprinkle with cheese.

Serving Suggestion: Serve with salad and crusty Italian bread.

Chick-Pea and Shrimp Soup

Italian Peasant Salad
Makes 6 servings

1 (6.9-ounce) package RICE-A-RONI® Chicken Flavor
2 tablespoons vegetable oil
1 (16-ounce) can cannellini beans, Great Northern beans or navy beans, rinsed
    and drained
2 cups chopped cooked chicken
2 medium tomatoes, chopped
1 cup frozen or canned peas, drained
½ cup Italian dressing
1 teaspoon dried basil *or* ½ teaspoon dried rosemary leaves, crushed

1. In large skillet over medium heat, sauté rice-vermicelli mix with oil until vermicelli is golden brown.

2. Slowly stir in 2½ cups water and Special Seasonings; bring to a boil. Reduce heat to low. Cover; simmer 15 to 20 minutes or until rice is tender. Cool 10 minutes.

3. In large bowl, combine rice mixture, beans, chicken, tomatoes, peas, Italian dressing and basil. Cover; chill 1 hour before serving.

Prep Time: 10 minutes
Cook Time: 25 minutes

Lentil Soup

Makes 6 servings

1 tablespoon FILIPPO BERIO® Olive Oil
1 medium onion, diced
4 cups beef broth
1 cup dried lentils, rinsed and drained
¼ cup tomato sauce
1 teaspoon dried Italian herb seasoning
  Salt and freshly ground black pepper

In large saucepan, heat olive oil over medium heat until hot. Add onion; cook and stir 5 minutes or until softened. Add beef broth; bring mixture to a boil. Stir in lentils, tomato sauce and Italian seasoning. Cover; reduce heat to low and simmer 45 minutes or until lentils are tender. Season to taste with salt and pepper. Serve hot.

Sicilian-Style Pasta Salad

Makes 10 servings

1 pound dry rotini pasta
2 cans (14.5 ounces each) CONTADINA® Recipe Ready Diced Tomatoes with
    Italian Herbs, undrained
1 cup sliced yellow bell pepper
1 cup sliced zucchini
8 ounces cooked bay shrimp
1 can (2.25 ounces) sliced pitted ripe olives, drained
2 tablespoons balsamic vinegar

1. Cook pasta according to package directions; drain.

2. Combine pasta, undrained tomatoes, bell pepper, zucchini, shrimp, olives and vinegar in large bowl; toss well.

3. Cover. Chill before serving.

Summer Minestrone with Pesto

Makes 8 (1-cup) servings

4 tablespoons olive oil, divided
2 cups diced carrots
3 medium zucchini and/or yellow squash, diced
1 jar (1 pound 10 ounces) RAGÚ® Light Pasta Sauce
2 cans (13¾ ounces each) chicken or vegetable broth
1 can (19 ounces) cannellini or white kidney beans, rinsed and drained
1 cup packed fresh basil leaves
1 large clove garlic, finely chopped
¼ teaspoon salt

In 5-quart saucepan, heat 1 tablespoon olive oil over medium-high heat and cook carrots and zucchini, stirring occasionally, 8 minutes. Stir in Ragú Light Pasta Sauce and chicken broth. Bring to a boil over high heat. Reduce heat to low and simmer covered, stirring occasionally, 20 minutes or until vegetables are tender. Stir in beans; heat through.

Meanwhile, for pesto, in blender or food processor, blend basil, garlic, salt and remaining 3 tablespoons oil until basil is finely chopped. To serve, ladle soup into bowls and garnish each with spoonful of pesto. Serve, if desired, with crusty Italian bread.

Prep Time: 20 minutes
Cook Time: 30 minutes

Summer Minestrone with Pesto

Tomato-Fresh Mozzarella Salad

Makes 4 servings

   Vinaigrette Dressing (recipe follows)
1 pound fresh mozzarella
1 pound ripe tomatoes
   Fresh whole large basil leaves as needed
   Salt and ground pepper

Prepare Vinaigrette Dressing. Cut mozzarella in ¼-inch slices. Cut tomatoes into ¼-inch slices. Alternate mozzarella slices, tomato slices and basil leaves, overlapping on plate. Drizzle with dressing; sprinkle with salt and pepper.

Vinaigrette Dressing

 1 tablespoon balsamic or wine vinegar
 ¼ teaspoon Dijon-style mustard
   Pinch salt, pepper and sugar
 ¼ cup olive oil

Whisk vinegar, mustard, salt, pepper and sugar in small bowl until smooth. Add oil in thin stream, whisking until dressing is smooth. Refrigerate until ready to use. Whisk again before serving.

Tomato-Fresh Mozzarella Salad

Pasta

Fettuccine alla Carbonara

Makes 4 servings

¾ pound uncooked fettuccine or spaghetti
4 ounces pancetta (Italian bacon) or lean American bacon, cut into ½-inch-wide
   strips
3 cloves garlic, cut into halves
¼ cup dry white wine
⅓ cup heavy or whipping cream
1 egg
1 egg yolk
⅔ cup freshly grated Parmesan cheese, divided
   Generous dash white pepper
   Fresh oregano leaves for garnish (optional)

1. Cook fettuccine according to package directions just until al dente; remove from heat. Drain well; return to dry pot.

2. Cook and stir pancetta and garlic in large skillet over medium-low heat 4 minutes or until pancetta is light brown. Reserve 2 tablespoons drippings in skillet with pancetta. Discard garlic and remaining drippings.

3. Add wine to pancetta mixture; cook over medium heat 3 minutes or until wine is almost evaporated. Stir in cream; cook and stir 2 minutes. Remove from heat.

4. Whisk egg and egg yolk in top of double boiler. Place top of double boiler over simmering water, adjusting heat to maintain simmer. Whisk ⅓ cup cheese and pepper into egg mixture; cook and stir until sauce thickens slightly.

5. Pour pancetta mixture over fettuccine in pot; toss to coat. Heat over medium-low heat until heated through. Stir in egg mixture. Toss to coat evenly. Remove from heat. Serve with remaining ⅓ cup cheese. Garnish with oregano, if desired.

Fettuccine alla Carbonara

DON'T USE DICED TOMATOES

Chicken and Linguine in Creamy Tomato Sauce

Makes 4 servings

1 tablespoon olive oil
1 pound boneless, skinless chicken breasts, cut into ½-inch strips
1 jar (1 pound 10 ounces) RAGÚ® Old World Style® Pasta Sauce
2 cups water
8 ounces linguine or spaghetti
½ cup whipping or heavy cream
1 tablespoon chopped fresh basil leaves *or* ½ teaspoon dried basil leaves, crushed

1. In 12-inch skillet, heat olive oil over medium heat and brown chicken. Remove chicken and set aside.

2. In same skillet, stir in Ragú Old World Style Pasta Sauce and water. Bring to a boil over high heat. Stir in uncooked linguine and return to a boil. Reduce heat to low and simmer covered, stirring occasionally, 15 minutes or until linguine is tender.

3. Stir in cream and basil. Return chicken to skillet and cook 5 minutes or until chicken is thoroughly cooked.

Prep Time: 10 minutes
Cook Time: 30 minutes

Chicken and Linguine in Creamy Tomato Sauce

61

Easy Cheesy Lasagna

Makes 6 servings

2 tablespoons olive oil
3 small zucchini, quartered and thinly sliced
1 package (8 ounces) mushrooms, thinly sliced
1 medium onion, chopped
5 cloves garlic, minced
2 containers (15 ounces each) ricotta cheese
2 eggs
¼ cup grated Parmesan cheese
½ teaspoon Italian seasoning
¼ teaspoon garlic salt
⅛ teaspoon black pepper
1 can (28 ounces) crushed tomatoes in purée, undrained
1 jar (26 ounces) pasta sauce
1 package (16 ounces) lasagna noodles, uncooked
4 cups (16 ounces) shredded mozzarella cheese, divided

1. Preheat oven to 375°F. Grease 13×9-inch baking dish or lasagna pan.

2. Heat oil in large skillet over medium heat until hot. Add zucchini, mushrooms, onion and garlic. Cook and stir 5 minutes or until vegetables are tender. Combine ricotta cheese, eggs, Parmesan cheese, Italian seasoning, garlic salt and pepper in medium bowl. Combine tomatoes and pasta sauce in another bowl.

3. Spread about ¾ cup tomato mixture in prepared dish. Place layer of noodles over tomato mixture, overlapping noodles. Spread half of vegetable mixture over noodles; top with half of ricotta mixture. Sprinkle with 1 cup mozzarella. Place second layer of noodles over mozzarella. Spread about 1 cup tomato mixture over noodles. Top with remaining vegetable and ricotta cheese mixtures. Sprinkle with 1 cup mozzarella. Top with third layer of noodles, remaining tomato mixture and remaining 2 cups mozzarella.

4. Cover tightly with foil and bake 1 hour or until noodles in center are soft. Uncover and bake 5 minutes or until cheese is melted and lightly browned. Remove from oven; cover and let stand 15 minutes before serving.

Hearty Manicotti

Roasted Garlic Orzo

Makes 8 to 10 servings

6 cloves garlic, unpeeled
2 medium onions, chopped
3 cups (8 ounces) sliced mushrooms
2 tablespoons olive oil
8 ounces BARILLA® Orzo
2 cups chicken broth
¼ cup chopped parsley
   Salt and pepper
2 tablespoons grated Parmesan cheese

1. Wrap garlic in foil; bake in 450°F oven about 15 minutes or until soft.

2. Cook and stir onions and mushrooms in olive oil in large skillet until golden brown and tender.

3. Meanwhile, cook orzo in water and chicken broth according to package directions; drain and transfer to serving bowl.

4. Remove garlic from foil packet; squeeze cloves from skins into small bowl and discard skins. Mash garlic with fork.

5. Stir garlic, vegetables and parsley into hot drained orzo. Add salt and pepper to taste. Sprinkle with cheese. Serve warm.

Tip: The word orzo actually means "barley," even though the shape of this pasta looks more like rice. It is available in the pasta sections of large supermarkets.

Milano Shrimp Fettuccine

Makes 3 to 4 servings

4 ounces egg or spinach fettuccine
½ pound medium shrimp, peeled and deveined
1 clove garlic, minced
1 tablespoon olive oil
1 can (14½ ounces) DEL MONTE® Diced Tomatoes with Basil,
      Garlic & Oregano
½ cup whipping cream
¼ cup sliced green onions

1. Cook pasta according to package directions; drain.

2. Cook shrimp and garlic in hot oil in large skillet over medium-high heat until shrimp are pink and opaque.

3. Stir in undrained tomatoes; simmer 5 minutes. Blend in cream and green onions; heat through. *Do not boil.* Serve over hot pasta.

Prep & Cook Time: 20 minutes

Pasta with Spinach and Ricotta

Makes 4 servings

8 ounces uncooked tri-colored rotini
1 box (10 ounces) frozen chopped spinach, thawed and drained
2 teaspoons minced garlic
1 cup ricotta cheese
¼ cup grated Parmesan cheese, divided

1. Cook pasta according to package directions; drain.

2. While pasta is cooking, coat skillet with nonstick cooking spray; heat over medium-low heat. Add spinach and garlic; cook and stir 5 minutes. Stir in ricotta cheese, half of Parmesan cheese and ½ cup water; season with salt and pepper to taste.

3. Add pasta to skillet; stir until well blended. Sprinkle with remaining Parmesan cheese.

Classic Stuffed Shells

Makes 8 servings

1 jar (1 pound 10 ounces) RAGÚ® Old World Style® Pasta Sauce, divided
2 pounds ricotta cheese
2 cups shredded mozzarella cheese (about 8 ounces)
¼ cup grated Parmesan cheese
3 eggs
1 tablespoon finely chopped fresh parsley
⅛ teaspoon ground black pepper
1 box (12 ounces) jumbo shells pasta, cooked and drained

Preheat oven to 350°F. In 13×9-inch baking pan, evenly spread 1 cup Ragú Old World Style Pasta Sauce; set aside.

In large bowl, combine cheeses, eggs, parsley and black pepper. Fill shells with cheese mixture, then arrange in baking pan. Evenly top with remaining sauce. Bake 45 minutes or until sauce is bubbling.

Recipe Tip: For a change of shape, substitute cooked and drained cannelloni or manicotti tubes for the jumbo shells. Use a teaspoon or pastry bag to fill the tubes from end to end, being careful not to overfill them.

Tip: Pasta should always be cooked in plenty of water at a fast boil. This allows the pasta to circulate during cooking so that all of it will be evenly cooked.

Classic Stuffed Shells

Quick Pasta Puttanesca

Makes 6 to 8 servings

    1 package (16 ounces) spaghetti or linguine, uncooked
    3 tablespoons plus 1 teaspoon olive oil, divided
  ¼ to 1 teaspoon red pepper flakes*
    2 cans (6 ounces each) chunk light tuna packed in water, drained
    1 tablespoon dried minced onion
    1 teaspoon minced garlic
    1 can (28 ounces) diced tomatoes, undrained
    1 can (8 ounces) tomato sauce
  24 pitted kalamata or ripe olives
    2 tablespoons capers, drained

For a mildly spicy dish, use ¼ teaspoon red pepper. For a very spicy dish, use 1 teaspoon red pepper.

1. Cook spaghetti according to package directions. Drain pasta; do not rinse. Return pasta to pan; add 1 teaspoon oil and toss to coat.

2. While pasta is cooking, heat remaining 3 tablespoons oil in large skillet over medium-high heat. Add red pepper flakes; cook and stir 1 to 2 minutes or until they sizzle. Add tuna; cook and stir 2 to 3 minutes. Add onion and garlic; cook and stir 1 minute. Add tomatoes with juice, tomato sauce, olives and capers. Cook over medium-high heat, stirring frequently, until sauce is heated through.

3. Add sauce to pasta; mix well.

Quick Pasta Puttanesca

Rigatoni Con Ricotta

Makes 12 servings

1 package (16 ounces) BARILLA® Rigatoni
2 eggs
1 container (15 ounces) ricotta cheese
¾ cup (3 ounces) grated Parmesan cheese
1 tablespoon dried parsley
2 jars (26 ounces each) BARILLA® Lasagna & Casserole Sauce or Marinara
  Pasta Sauce, divided
3 cups (12 ounces) shredded mozzarella cheese, divided

1. Preheat oven to 375°F. Spray 13×9×2-inch baking pan with nonstick cooking spray. Cook rigatoni according to package directions; drain.

2. Beat eggs in small bowl. Stir in ricotta, Parmesan and parsley.

3. To assemble casserole, spread 2 cups lasagna sauce to cover bottom of pan. Place half of cooked rigatoni over sauce; top with half of ricotta mixture, dropped by spoonfuls. Layer with 1 cup mozzarella, 2 cups lasagna sauce, remaining rigatoni and ricotta mixture. Top with 1 cup mozzarella, remaining lasagna sauce and remaining 1 cup mozzarella.

4. Cover with foil and bake 60 to 70 minutes or until bubbly. Uncover and continue cooking about 5 minutes or until cheese is melted. Let stand 15 minutes before serving.

Rigatoni Con Ricotta

Orzo with Spinach and Red Pepper

Makes 6 servings

4 ounces uncooked orzo
1 teaspoon olive oil
1 medium red bell pepper, diced
3 cloves garlic, minced
1 package (10 ounces) frozen chopped spinach, thawed and squeezed dry
¼ cup grated Parmesan cheese
½ teaspoon minced fresh oregano or basil (optional)
¼ teaspoon lemon pepper

1. Prepare orzo according to package directions; drain well and set aside.

2. Spray large nonstick skillet with nonstick cooking spray. Heat skillet over medium-high heat until hot and add oil, tilting skillet to coat bottom. Add bell pepper and garlic; cook and stir 2 to 3 minutes or until bell pepper is crisp-tender. Add orzo and spinach; stir until evenly mixed and heated through. Remove from heat and stir in Parmesan cheese, oregano, if desired, and lemon pepper. Garnish as desired.

Linguine with Oil and Garlic

Makes 4 servings

½ cup FILIPPO BERIO® Extra Virgin Olive Oil, divided
10 cloves garlic, minced
¾ pound uncooked linguine
¼ teaspoon black pepper
¼ teaspoon salt (optional)

1. Heat 2 tablespoons olive oil in small saucepan over medium heat. Add garlic; cook and stir until lightly browned. Remove from heat; set aside.

2. Cook linguine according to package directions until tender. Do not overcook.

3. Drain pasta; return to saucepan. Toss with garlic and olive oil mixture, remaining 6 tablespoons olive oil, pepper and salt, if desired.

Orzo with Spinach and Red Pepper

Italian Garden Fusilli

Makes 6 to 8 servings

8 ounces dry fusilli
1 can (14.5 ounces) CONTADINA® Recipe Ready Diced Tomatoes, undrained
1 cup cut fresh green beans
½ teaspoon garlic salt
¼ teaspoon dried rosemary leaves, crushed
1 small zucchini, thinly sliced (about 1 cup)
1 small yellow squash, thinly sliced (about 1 cup)
1 jar (12 ounces) marinated artichoke hearts, undrained
1 cup frozen peas
½ teaspoon salt, or to taste
¼ teaspoon ground black pepper, or to taste
¼ cup (1 ounce) shredded Parmesan cheese

1. Cook pasta according to package directions; drain and keep warm.

2. Meanwhile, combine undrained tomatoes, green beans, garlic salt and rosemary in large skillet. Bring to a boil. Reduce heat to low; cover. Simmer for 3 minutes.

3. Add zucchini and yellow squash; cover. Simmer for 3 minutes or until vegetables are tender.

4. Stir in artichoke hearts and juice, peas, salt and pepper; heat through.

5. Add pasta; toss to coat well. Sprinkle with Parmesan cheese just before serving.

Prep Time: 10 minutes
Cook Time: 10 minutes

Italian Garden Fusilli

Classic Pesto with Linguine

Makes 4 servings (about ¾ cup pesto sauce)

¾ **pound uncooked linguine**
2 **tablespoons butter**
¼ **cup plus 1 tablespoon olive oil, divided**
2 **tablespoons pine nuts**
1 **cup tightly packed fresh (not dried) basil leaves, rinsed, drained and stemmed**
2 **cloves garlic**
¼ **teaspoon salt**
¼ **cup freshly grated Parmesan cheese**
1½ **tablespoons freshly grated Romano cheese**
   Fresh basil leaves for garnish (optional)

1. Prepare linguine according to package directions; drain. Toss with butter in large serving bowl; set aside and keep warm.

2. Heat 1 tablespoon oil in small saucepan or skillet over medium-low heat. Add pine nuts; cook and stir 30 to 45 seconds until light brown, shaking pan constantly. Remove with slotted spoon; drain on paper towels.

3. Place toasted pine nuts, basil leaves, garlic and salt in food processor or blender. With processor running, add remaining ¼ cup oil in slow steady stream until evenly blended and pine nuts are finely chopped.

4. Transfer basil mixture to small bowl. Stir in Parmesan and Romano cheeses.*

5. Combine hot buttered linguine and pesto sauce in large serving bowl; toss until well coated. Garnish, if desired. Serve immediately.

*Pesto sauce can be stored at this point in airtight container; pour thin layer of olive oil over pesto and cover. Refrigerate up to 1 week. Bring to room temperature. Proceed as directed in step 5.

Classic Pesto with Linguine

Chunky Pasta Sauce with Meat

Makes 4 servings (4 cups sauce)

6 ounces ground beef
6 ounces mild or hot Italian sausage, sliced
½ medium onion, coarsely chopped
1 clove garlic, minced
2 cans (14½ ounces each) DEL MONTE® Diced Tomatoes with Basil,
    Garlic & Oregano
1 can (8 ounces) DEL MONTE® Tomato Sauce
¼ cup red wine (optional)
    Hot cooked pasta
    Grated Parmesan cheese

1. Brown beef and sausage in large saucepan; drain all but 1 tablespoon drippings.

2. Add onion and garlic; cook until tender.

3. Add undrained tomatoes, tomato sauce and wine. Simmer, uncovered, 15 minutes, stirring frequently. Serve over pasta; top with Parmesan cheese.

Variation: Serve sauce over vegetables, omelets or frittatas.

Prep Time: 5 minutes
Cook Time: 25 minutes

Tip: Chunky sauces like this one are best served with
sturdy-shaped pastas such as rotini, penne, fusilli
or radiatore. The irregularities in their shapes
make them better able to hold on to the sauce.

Pasta with Beans & Broccoli Rabe

Makes 4 servings

  1 tablespoon olive oil
  1 tablespoon minced garlic
  1 pound broccoli rabe, washed, stemmed and coarsely chopped
  1 can (15½ ounces) cannellini beans, undrained
  1 cup chicken broth
  1 tablespoon *Frank's® RedHot®* Original Cayenne Pepper Sauce
 1⅓ cups *French's®* French Fried Onions, divided
  4 cups cooked rigatoni or campanelli pasta (about 3 cups uncooked)
   Grated Parmesan cheese

1. Heat oil in 12-inch nonstick skillet over high heat. Add garlic and sauté until golden. Add broccoli rabe and sauté 5 minutes or until tender. Stir in beans, broth and **Frank's RedHot** Sauce.

2. Bring to a boil over high heat. Reduce heat to medium-low; simmer 5 minutes, stirring frequently. Stir in ⅔ *cup* French Fried Onions and pasta; toss to coat.

3. Transfer to serving dish. Sprinkle with remaining onions and Parmesan cheese.

Prep Time: 10 minutes
Cook Time: about 15 minutes

Lasagna Florentine
Makes 8 servings

2 tablespoons olive oil
3 medium carrots, finely chopped
1 package (8 to 10 ounces) sliced mushrooms
1 medium onion, finely chopped
2 cloves garlic, finely chopped
1 jar (1 pound 10 ounces) RAGÚ® Robusto! Pasta Sauce
1 container (15 ounces) ricotta cheese
2 cups shredded mozzarella cheese, divided
1 box (10 ounces) frozen chopped spinach, thawed and squeezed dry
¼ cup grated Parmesan cheese
2 eggs
1 teaspoon salt
1 teaspoon dried Italian seasoning
16 lasagna noodles, cooked and drained

Preheat oven to 375°F. In 12-inch skillet, heat olive oil over medium heat and cook carrots, mushrooms, onion and garlic until carrots are almost tender, about 5 minutes. Stir in Ragú Robusto! Pasta Sauce; heat through.

Meanwhile, in medium bowl, combine ricotta cheese, 1½ cups mozzarella cheese, spinach, Parmesan cheese, eggs, salt and Italian seasoning; set aside.

In 13×9-inch baking dish, evenly spread ½ cup sauce mixture. Arrange 4 lasagna noodles, lengthwise over sauce, overlapping edges slightly. Spread ⅓ of the ricotta mixture over noodles; repeat layers, ending with noodles. Top with remaining sauce and ½ cup mozzarella cheese. Cover with foil and bake 40 minutes. Remove foil and continue baking 10 minutes or until bubbling.

Lasagna Florentine

Spaghetti with Tomatoes and Olives

Makes 6 to 8 servings

2 tablespoons extra-virgin olive oil
3 cloves garlic, finely chopped
1½ pounds fresh ripe tomatoes, seeded and chopped (about 3 cups)
1 tablespoon tomato paste
1 teaspoon dried oregano
⅛ teaspoon ground red pepper
½ cup pitted brine-cured black olives, coarsely chopped
2 tablespoons capers
Salt and pepper
1 package (16 ounces) BARILLA® Thin Spaghetti
Grated Parmesan cheese

1. Heat olive oil and garlic in large skillet over low heat until garlic begins to sizzle. Add tomatoes, tomato paste, oregano and red pepper; simmer, uncovered, until sauce is thickened, about 15 minutes. Add olives, capers and salt and pepper to taste.

2. Meanwhile, cook spaghetti according to package directions; drain.

3. Toss spaghetti with sauce. Sprinkle with cheese before serving.

Tip: To seed a tomato, cut it in half crosswise. Holding each tomato half over a bowl, gently squeeze the tomato to remove the seeds.

Spaghetti with Tomatoes and Olives

Zesty Artichoke Pesto Sauce

Makes 6 to 8 servings

1 jar (6 ounces) marinated artichoke hearts, chopped, marinade reserved
1 cup sliced onion
1 can (14.5 ounces) CONTADINA® Recipe Ready Diced Tomatoes, undrained
1 can (6 ounces) CONTADINA® Italian Paste with Tomato Pesto
1 cup water
½ teaspoon salt
  Hot cooked pasta

1. Heat reserved artichoke marinade in large saucepan over medium-high heat until warm.

2. Add onion; cook for 3 to 4 minutes or until tender. Add artichoke hearts, tomatoes and juice, tomato paste, water and salt.

3. Bring to a boil; reduce heat to low. Cook, stirring occasionally, for 10 to 15 minutes or until flavors are blended. Serve over pasta.

Savory Caper and Olive Sauce: Eliminate artichoke hearts. Heat 2 tablespoons olive oil in large saucepan over medium-high heat. Add onion; cook for 3 to 4 minutes or until tender. Add tomatoes and juice, tomato paste, water, salt, ¾ cup sliced and quartered zucchini, ½ cup (2¼-ounce can) drained sliced ripe olives and 2 tablespoons capers. Proceed as above.

Prep Time: 5 minutes
Cook Time: 19 minutes

Mushroom Ragoût with Polenta

Garden-Style Risotto
Makes 6 servings

1 can (14½ ounces) low-sodium chicken broth
1¾ cups water
2 garlic cloves, finely chopped
1 teaspoon dried basil leaves, crushed
½ teaspoon dried thyme leaves, crushed
1 cup arborio rice
2 cups packed DOLE® Fresh Spinach, torn
1 cup DOLE® Shredded Carrots
3 tablespoons grated Parmesan cheese

• Combine broth, water, garlic, basil and thyme in large saucepan. Bring to a boil; meanwhile, prepare rice.

• Place rice in large, nonstick saucepan sprayed with vegetable cooking spray. Cook and stir rice over medium heat about 2 minutes or until rice is browned.

• Pour 1 cup boiling broth into saucepan with rice; cook, stirring constantly, until broth is almost absorbed (there should be some broth left).

• Add enough broth to barely cover rice; continue to cook, stirring constantly, until broth is almost absorbed. Repeat adding broth and cooking, stirring constantly, until broth is almost absorbed, about 15 minutes; add spinach and carrots with the last addition of broth.

• Cook 3 to 5 minutes more, stirring constantly, or until broth is almost absorbed and rice and vegetables are tender. Do not overcook. (Risotto will be saucy and have a creamy texture.) Stir in Parmesan cheese. Serve warm.

Garden Pilaf: Substitute 1 cup uncooked long grain white rice for arborio rice and reduce water from 1¾ cups to ½ cup. Prepare broth as directed above with ½ cup water; meanwhile, brown rice as directed above. Carefully add browned rice to boiling broth. Reduce heat to low; cover and cook 15 minutes. Stir in vegetables; cover and cook 4 to 5 minutes longer or until rice and vegetables are tender. Stir in Parmesan cheese.

Garden-Style Risotto

Parmesan Polenta

Makes 6 servings

 4 cups chicken broth
 1 small onion, minced
 4 cloves garlic, minced
 1 tablespoon minced fresh rosemary *or* 1 teaspoon dried rosemary leaves
 ½ teaspoon salt
1¼ cups yellow cornmeal
 6 tablespoons grated Parmesan cheese
 1 tablespoon olive oil, divided

1. Spray 11×7-inch baking pan with nonstick cooking spray; set aside. Spray one side of 7-inch-long sheet of waxed paper with cooking spray; set aside.

2. Combine chicken broth, onion, garlic, rosemary and salt in medium saucepan. Bring to a boil over high heat; add cornmeal gradually, stirring constantly. Reduce heat to medium and simmer 30 minutes or until mixture has consistency of thick mashed potatoes. Remove from heat and stir in cheese.

3. Spread polenta evenly in prepared pan; place waxed paper, sprayed-side down, on polenta and smooth. (If surface is bumpy, it is more likely to stick to grill.) Cool on wire rack 15 minutes or until firm. Remove waxed paper; cut into 6 squares. Remove squares from pan.

4. To prevent sticking, spray grid with cooking spray. Prepare coals for grilling. Brush tops of squares with half the oil. Grill oil-side down on covered grill over medium to low coals for 6 to 8 minutes or until golden. Brush with remaining oil and gently turn over. Grill 6 to 8 minutes more or until golden. Serve warm.

Parmesan Polenta

Risotto alla Milanese

Makes 6 to 8 servings

¼ teaspoon saffron threads
3½ to 4 cups chicken broth
7 tablespoons butter or margarine, divided
1 large onion, chopped
1½ cups uncooked arborio or short-grain white rice
½ cup dry white wine
½ teaspoon salt
Dash pepper
¼ cup freshly grated Parmesan cheese
Chopped fresh parsley and tomato slices for garnish (optional)

1. Crush saffron in mortar with pestle to a powder. Place saffron in glass measuring cup.

2. Bring broth to a boil in small saucepan over medium heat; reduce heat to low. Stir ½ cup broth into saffron to dissolve. Keep remaining broth hot.

3. Heat 6 tablespoons butter in large, heavy skillet or 2½-quart saucepan over medium heat until melted and bubbly. Cook and stir onion in hot butter 5 minutes or until onion is soft. Stir in rice; cook and stir 2 minutes. Stir in wine, salt and pepper. Cook, uncovered, over medium-high heat 3 to 5 minutes until wine has evaporated, stirring occasionally.

4. Measure ½ cup hot broth; stir into rice mixture. Reduce heat to medium-low, maintaining a simmer throughout steps 4 and 5. Cook and stir until broth has absorbed. Repeat, adding ½ cup broth 3 more times, cooking and stirring until broth has absorbed.

5. Add saffron-flavored broth to rice and cook until absorbed. Continue adding remaining broth, ½ cup at a time, cooking and stirring until rice is tender but firm and mixture has slightly creamy consistency. (Not all the broth may be necessary. Total cooking time of rice will be about 20 minutes.)

6. Remove risotto from heat. Stir in remaining 1 tablespoon butter and cheese. Garnish, if desired. Serve immediately.

Risotto alla Milanese

Wild Mushroom Risotto
Makes 4 servings

1 cup sliced portobello mushrooms
1 cup sliced shiitake mushrooms, stems discarded
½ cup finely chopped onion
2 tablespoons *French's®* Worcestershire Sauce
2 cups uncooked arborio rice or white rice
2 cans (10½ ounces each) condensed chicken broth
½ cup frozen baby peas
½ cup (2 ounces) grated Parmesan cheese

1. Heat *1 tablespoon oil* in 5-quart saucepot or Dutch oven over medium-high heat. Add mushrooms and onion. Cook and stir 3 minutes or until mushrooms are tender. Add Worcestershire. Cook, stirring, until liquid is absorbed.

2. Add rice; cook 2 minutes, stirring constantly. Combine broth and *2½ cups water*. Add *4 cups* liquid to rice. Heat to boiling. Reduce heat to medium-low. Cook, uncovered, 8 minutes or until liquid is absorbed, stirring often. Add remaining broth, *½ cup* at a time. Cook and stir until rice is firm but tender and creamy.

3. Stir in peas and cheese; cook 1 minute. Serve with tossed green salad, if desired.

Prep Time: 5 minutes
Cook Time: about 15 minutes

Tip: *Portobello and shiitake mushrooms are both large, dark brown mushrooms used in a wide variety of dishes. They have dense, meaty flesh and tough woody stems that should be removed before cooking.*

BelGioioso® Parmesan Polenta

Makes 4 to 6 servings

Nonstick vegetable oil spray
4 cups canned vegetable broth
1½ cups yellow cornmeal
¾ cup grated BELGIOIOSO® Parmesan Cheese (about 2 ounces)

Preheat oven to 375°F. Spray 8×8×2-inch glass baking dish with vegetable oil spray. Bring vegetable broth to a boil in medium heavy saucepan over medium heat. Gradually whisk in cornmeal. Continue to whisk until mixture is very thick, about 3 minutes. Mix in BelGioioso Parmesan Cheese and pour mixture into prepared dish. Bake polenta until top begins to brown, about 30 minutes. Serve hot.

Sausage and Polenta Casserole

Makes 4 servings

1 tablespoon olive oil
1 cup chopped mushrooms
1 small red bell pepper, seeded and diced
1 small onion, diced
1 pound hot or mild bulk Italian sausage
1 jar (28 to 30 ounces) meatless pasta sauce
1 roll (16 to 18 ounces) polenta

1. Preheat oven to 350°F.

2. Heat oil in large skillet. Add mushrooms, bell pepper and onion; cook and stir over medium heat 5 minutes or until tender. Add sausage; cook and stir until sausage is brown, breaking into small pieces with spoon. Drain. Stir in pasta sauce and simmer 5 minutes.

3. Cut polenta roll into 9 slices and arrange in greased 9-inch square casserole. Top with sausage mixture.

4. Bake 15 minutes or until heated through.

Peasant Risotto

Makes 4 servings

1 teaspoon olive oil
3 ounces chopped ham
2 cloves garlic, minced
1 cup arborio or white short-grain rice
1 can (15 ounces) Great Northern beans, rinsed and drained
¼ cup chopped green onions with tops
½ teaspoon dried sage leaves
2 cans (14 ounces each) reduced-sodium chicken broth, heated
1½ cups Swiss chard, rinsed, stems removed and shredded
¼ cup freshly grated Parmesan cheese

1. Heat oil in large saucepan over medium heat. Add ham and garlic. Cook and stir until garlic is browned. Add rice, beans, green onions and sage; mix well. Add warm broth; bring to a boil. Reduce heat to low. Cook about 25 minutes or until rice is creamy, stirring frequently.

2. Add Swiss chard and Parmesan; mix well. Cover; remove from heat. Let stand, covered, 2 minutes or until Swiss chard is wilted. Serve immediately.

Tip: *Arborio is an Italian-grown variety of short grain rice with a very high starch content. It is the traditional choice for making risotto, as the increased amount of starch in the grains gives the finished dish its creamy texture.*

Peasant Risotto

Polenta Triangles
Makes 8 servings

½ cup yellow corn grits
1½ cups reduced-sodium chicken broth, divided
2 cloves garlic, minced
½ cup (2 ounces) crumbled feta cheese
1 red bell pepper, roasted,* peeled and finely chopped

Place pepper on foil-lined broiler pan; broil 15 minutes or until blackened on all sides, turning every 5 minutes. Place pepper in paper bag; close bag and let stand 15 minutes before peeling.

1. Combine grits and ½ cup chicken broth in small bowl; mix well and set aside. Pour remaining 1 cup broth into large heavy saucepan; bring to a boil. Add garlic and moistened grits; mix well and return to a boil. Reduce heat to low; cover and cook 20 minutes. Remove from heat; add feta cheese. Stir until cheese is completely melted. Add bell pepper; mix well.

2. Spray 8-inch square pan with nonstick cooking spray. Spoon grits mixture into prepared pan. Press grits evenly into pan with wet fingertips. Refrigerate until cold.

3. Spray grid with nonstick cooking spray. Prepare grill for direct cooking. Turn polenta out onto cutting board and cut into 2-inch squares. Cut each square diagonally into 2 triangles.

4. Place polenta triangles on grid. Grill over medium-high heat 1 minute or until bottoms are lightly browned. Turn triangles over and grill until browned and crisp. Serve warm or at room temperature.

Polenta Triangles

Risotto-Style Primavera
Makes 4 servings

1 tablespoon FILIPPO BERIO® Olive Oil
1 small zucchini, sliced
1 medium onion, sliced
½ red bell pepper, seeded and cut into thin strips
3 mushrooms, sliced
½ cup uncooked long grain rice
¼ cup dry white wine
1 cup chicken broth
1¾ cups water, divided
2 tablespoons grated Parmesan cheese
   Salt and freshly ground black pepper

In large saucepan or skillet, heat olive oil over medium heat until hot. Add zucchini, onion, bell pepper and mushrooms. Cook and stir 5 to 7 minutes or until zucchini is tender-crisp. Remove vegetables; set aside. Add rice and wine; stir until wine is absorbed. Add chicken broth. Cook, uncovered, stirring frequently, until absorbed. Add 1 cup water. Cook, uncovered, stirring frequently, until absorbed. Add remaining ¾ cup water. Cook, uncovered, stirring frequently, until absorbed. (Total cook time will be about 25 minutes until rice is tender and mixture is creamy.) Stir in vegetables and Parmesan cheese. Season to taste with salt and black pepper

Tip: Choose zucchini that are heavy for their size, firm and well shaped. They should have a bright color and be free of cuts and any soft spots. Small zucchini are more tender because they have been harvested when they were young. They should be rinsed well before using, but peeling is not necessary.

Risotto-Style Primavera

Polenta with Pasta Sauce & Vegetables

Makes 4 servings

    1 can (14½ ounces) reduced-sodium chicken broth
1½ cups water
    1 cup yellow cornmeal
    2 teaspoons olive oil
  12 ounces assorted cut vegetables, such as broccoli florets, bell peppers, red
        onions, zucchini squash and thin carrot strips
    2 teaspoons minced garlic
    2 cups prepared tomato-basil pasta sauce
  ½ cup grated Asiago cheese
  ¼ cup chopped fresh basil (optional)

1. To prepare polenta, whisk together chicken broth, water and cornmeal
in large microwavable bowl. Cover with waxed paper; microwave at HIGH
5 minutes. Whisk well and microwave at HIGH 4 to 5 minutes more or until
polenta is very thick. Whisk again; cover and keep warm.

2. Meanwhile, heat oil in large deep nonstick skillet over medium heat. Add
vegetables and garlic; cook and stir 5 minutes. Add pasta sauce; reduce heat.
Cover and simmer 5 to 8 minutes or until vegetables are tender.

3. Spoon polenta onto serving plates; top with pasta sauce mixture. Sprinkle
with cheese and basil, if desired.

Prep Time: 5 minutes
Cook Time: 15 minutes

Polenta with Pasta Sauce & Vegetables

Classic Risotto
Makes 4 servings

1 can (14½ ounces) chicken broth
2 cups water
¼ cup I CAN'T BELIEVE IT'S NOT BUTTER!® Spread
1 small onion, chopped
1 clove garlic, finely chopped
1 cup uncooked arborio or long grain rice
¼ cup dry white wine or chicken broth
¼ cup grated Parmesan cheese
1 tablespoon finely chopped fresh parsley (optional)

In 2-quart saucepan, bring broth and water to a boil; set aside.

In another 2-quart saucepan, melt I Can't Believe It's Not Butter!® Spread over medium-high heat and cook onion and garlic, stirring occasionally, 2 minutes or until onion is tender. Stir in uncooked rice and cook, stirring occasionally, 2 minutes or until rice is golden. Stir in wine and cook 1 minute or until liquid is absorbed. Reduce heat to low and add hot broth mixture, ½ cup at a time, stirring constantly, until liquid is absorbed and rice is slightly creamy and just tender. Stir in cheese and parsley.

Tip: Avoid buying pregrated Parmesan cheese if possible—the flavor of freshly grated is far superior. Both domestic and imported Parmesan cheeses are sold in chunks and wedges at supermarkets and Italian specialty stores, and these can be quickly grated by hand with a four-sided or rotary grater.

Chicken Tuscany

Italian-Glazed Pork Chops

Makes 8 servings

  1 tablespoon olive oil
  8 bone-in pork chops
  1 medium zucchini, thinly sliced
  1 medium red bell pepper, chopped
  1 medium onion, thinly sliced
  3 cloves garlic, finely chopped
  ¼ cup dry red wine or beef broth
  1 jar (1 pound 10 ounces) RAGÚ® Chunky Gardenstyle Pasta Sauce

1. In 12-inch skillet, heat olive oil over medium-high heat and brown chops. Remove chops and set aside.

2. In same skillet, cook zucchini, red bell pepper, onion and garlic, stirring occasionally, 4 minutes. Stir in wine and Ragú Chunky Gardenstyle Pasta Sauce.

3. Return chops to skillet, turning to coat with sauce. Simmer covered 15 minutes or until chops are tender and barely pink in the center. Serve, if desired, over hot cooked couscous or rice.

Prep Time: 10 minutes
Cook Time: 25 minutes

Tip: After purchasing pork chops, store them in the coldest part of the refrigerator (on the bottom shelf) for 2 to 3 days. If they are wrapped in butcher paper, they should be rewrapped in plastic wrap to prevent juices from escaping.

Italian-Glazed Pork Chop

Beef Sirloin in Rich Italian Sauce

Makes 4 servings

   2 tablespoons olive or vegetable oil
   1 pound top sirloin, cut into thin strips
   2 cloves garlic, cut in half
   1 can (14.5 ounces) CONTADINA® Recipe Ready Diced Tomatoes, undrained
   2 tablespoons chopped fresh parsley *or* 2 teaspoons dried parsley flakes
   2 tablespoons dry red wine or beef broth
   ½ teaspoon dried thyme leaves, crushed
   ¼ teaspoon dried rosemary leaves, crushed
   ¼ teaspoon salt
   ¼ teaspoon ground black pepper
     Additional chopped fresh parsley (optional)

1. Heat oil over high heat in large skillet. Add meat and garlic; cook for 1 to 2 minutes or until meat is browned, stirring occasionally. Remove meat from skillet; discard garlic.

2. Add undrained tomatoes, parsley, wine, thyme, rosemary, salt and pepper to skillet; stir. Bring to a boil. Reduce heat to low.

3. Return meat to skillet; cover. Simmer for 5 minutes. Sprinkle with additional fresh parsley, if desired.

Prep Time: 8 minutes
Cook Time: 9 minutes

Pork Spiedini
Makes 6 servings

2 pounds boneless pork loin, cut into 1-inch cubes
¾ cup cider vinegar
¾ cup olive oil
4 tablespoons lemon juice
1 tablespoon Worcestershire sauce
1 tablespoon dried oregano
2 cloves garlic, minced
2 teaspoons ground black pepper
1 teaspoon salt
1 teaspoon dried thyme
½ teaspoon cayenne pepper
6 thick slices Italian bread

Combine all ingredients, except bread, in resealable plastic food storage bag; refrigerate 4 to 24 hours. Remove pork cubes from marinade; thread pork onto skewers. (If using bamboo skewers, soak in water for 1 hour to prevent burning.) Grill over hot coals, basting with reserved marinade, for 4 to 5 minutes; discard marinade. Turn kabobs and grill 4 minutes. Serve by pulling meat off of skewer onto Italian bread.

Prep Time: 15 minutes
Cook Time: 10 minutes

Favorite recipe from **National Pork Board**

Poached Seafood Italiano

Makes 4 servings

1 tablespoon olive or vegetable oil
1 large clove garlic, minced
¼ cup dry white wine or chicken broth
4 (6-ounce) salmon steaks or fillets
1 can (14.5 ounces) CONTADINA® Recipe Ready Diced Tomatoes
    with Italian Herbs, undrained
⅓ cup sliced olives (black, green or a combination)
2 tablespoons chopped fresh basil (optional)

1. Heat oil in large skillet. Add garlic; sauté 30 seconds. Add wine. Bring to a boil.

2. Add salmon; cover. Reduce heat to medium; simmer 6 minutes.

3. Add undrained tomatoes and olives; simmer 2 minutes or until salmon flakes easily when tested with fork. Sprinkle with basil just before serving, if desired.

Grilled Italian Steak

Makes 8 servings

¾ cup WISH-BONE® Italian Dressing*
2 tablespoons grated Parmesan cheese
2 teaspoons dried basil leaves, crushed
¼ teaspoon cracked black pepper
1 (2- to 3-pound) boneless sirloin or top round steak

Also terrific with WISH-BONE® Robusto Italian or Just 2 Good! Italian Dressing.

In large, shallow nonaluminum baking dish or plastic bag, combine all ingredients except steak. Add steak; turn to coat. Cover or close bag and marinate in refrigerator, turning occasionally, 3 to 24 hours.

Remove steak from marinade, reserving marinade. Grill or broil steak, turning once, until steak is done.

Meanwhile, in small saucepan, bring reserved marinade to a boil and continue boiling 1 minute. Pour over steak.

Poached Seafood Italiano

Chicken Cacciatore
Makes 4 servings

8 ounces uncooked pasta
1 can (15 ounces) chunky Italian-style tomato sauce
1 cup chopped green bell pepper
1 cup sliced onion
1 cup sliced mushrooms
   Nonstick cooking spray
4 boneless skinless chicken breasts (about 1 pound)
   Salt and pepper

1. Cook pasta according to package directions; drain.

2. While pasta is cooking, combine tomato sauce, bell pepper, onion and mushrooms in microwavable dish. Cover loosely with plastic wrap or waxed paper; microwave at HIGH 6 to 8 minutes, stirring halfway through cooking time.

3. While sauce mixture is cooking, coat large skillet with cooking spray and heat over medium-high heat. Cook chicken breasts 3 to 4 minutes per side or until lightly browned.

4. Add sauce mixture to skillet; season with salt and pepper. Reduce heat to medium and simmer 12 to 15 minutes. Serve over pasta.

Tip: Cacciatore, Italian for "hunter," refers to dishes prepared "hunter's style," containing tomatoes, mushrooms, onions, herbs and sometimes wine.

Chicken Cacciatore

Rosemary Steak
Makes 4 servings

4 boneless beef top loin (New York strip) steaks (about 6 ounces each)
2 tablespoons minced fresh rosemary
2 cloves garlic, minced
1 tablespoon extra-virgin olive oil
1 teaspoon grated lemon peel
1 teaspoon coarsely ground black pepper
½ teaspoon salt
    Fresh rosemary sprigs

Score steaks in diamond pattern on both sides. Combine minced rosemary, garlic, oil, lemon peel, pepper and salt in small bowl; rub mixture onto surface of meat. Cover and refrigerate at least 15 minutes. Grill steaks over medium-hot KINGSFORD® Briquets about 4 minutes per side until medium-rare or to desired doneness. Cut steaks diagonally into ½-inch-thick slices. Garnish with rosemary sprigs.

Tip: Extra-virgin olive oil is considered the highest quality available. It results from the first pressing of olives which are cold pressed (a method that uses only pressure and no chemicals), producing a fruity, intensely flavored oil with a very low level of acidity.

Rosemary Steak

Italian Eggplant Parmigiana
Makes 4 servings

1 large eggplant, sliced ¼ inch thick
2 eggs, beaten
½ cup dry bread crumbs
1 can (14½ ounces) DEL MONTE® Stewed Tomatoes - Seasoned with Basil,
    Garlic & Oregano
1 can (15 ounces) DEL MONTE® Tomato Sauce
2 cloves garlic, minced
½ teaspoon dried basil
6 ounces mozzarella cheese, sliced

1. Dip eggplant slices into eggs, then bread crumbs; arrange in single layer on baking sheet. Broil 4 inches from heat until brown and tender, about 5 minutes per side.

2. Reduce oven temperature to 350°F. Place eggplant in 13×9-inch baking dish.

3. Combine tomatoes, tomato sauce, garlic and basil; pour over eggplant and top with cheese.

4. Cover and bake at 350°F 30 minutes or until heated through. Sprinkle with grated Parmesan cheese, if desired.

Prep Time: 15 minutes
Cook Time: 30 minutes

Red Snapper Scampi
Makes 4 servings

¼ cup butter, softened
1 tablespoon white wine
1½ teaspoons minced garlic
½ teaspoon grated lemon peel
⅛ teaspoon black pepper
1½ pounds red snapper, orange roughy or grouper fillets

1. Preheat oven to 450°F. Combine butter, wine, garlic, lemon peel and pepper in small bowl; stir to blend.

2. Place fish on foil-lined shallow baking pan. Top with seasoned butter. Bake 10 to 12 minutes or until fish begins to flake easily when tested with fork.

Tip: Serve fish over mixed salad greens, if desired. Or, add sliced carrots, zucchini and bell pepper cut into matchstick-size strips to the fish in the baking pan for an easy vegetable side dish.

Chicken Pomodoro with Tomato Basil Garlic
Makes 8 servings

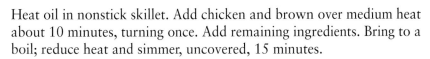

4 teaspoons olive oil
8 boneless skinless chicken breast halves
8 ounces fresh mushrooms, sliced
2 cans (14¼ ounces each) Italian-style stewed tomatoes
8 teaspoons MRS. DASH® Tomato Basil Garlic Seasoning
½ cup semi-dry white wine (optional)

Heat oil in nonstick skillet. Add chicken and brown over medium heat about 10 minutes, turning once. Add remaining ingredients. Bring to a boil; reduce heat and simmer, uncovered, 15 minutes.

Prep Time: 10 minutes
Cook Time: 25 minutes

129

Chicken Marsala

Makes 4 servings

1 tablespoon butter
2 boneless skinless chicken breasts, halved
1 cup sliced carrots
1 cup sliced fresh mushrooms
⅓ cup chicken broth
⅓ cup HOLLAND HOUSE® Marsala Cooking Wine

Melt butter in skillet over medium-high heat. Add chicken; cook 5 minutes. Turn chicken over; add remaining ingredients. Bring to a boil; simmer 15 to 20 minutes until juices run clear. Serve over cooked fettuccine, if desired.

Veal Piccata

Makes 4 servings

1 pound veal cutlets (or chicken)
2 garlic cloves, crushed
   All-purpose flour
2 tablespoons oil
4 tablespoons butter, divided
½ cup HOLLAND HOUSE® Vermouth Cooking Wine
2 tablespoons lemon juice
1 tablespoon chopped fresh parsley
   Freshly ground pepper

1. Rub veal or chicken with garlic; coat with flour. Heat oil and 2 tablespoons butter in large skillet over medium heat. Add veal; brown on both sides until cooked through. Transfer to serving platter; keep warm.

2. In small saucepan, combine cooking wine, remaining 2 tablespoons butter, lemon juice, parsley and pepper. Bring to boil, stirring constantly. Cook 1 minute over high heat. Pour sauce over veal.

Chicken Marsala

Spicy Shrimp Puttanesca

Makes 4 servings

    8 ounces uncooked linguine, capellini or spaghetti
    1 tablespoon olive oil
   12 ounces medium shrimp, peeled and deveined
    4 cloves garlic, minced
   ¾ teaspoon red pepper flakes
    1 cup finely chopped onion
    1 can (14½ ounces) no-salt-added stewed tomatoes, undrained
    2 tablespoons tomato paste
    2 tablespoons chopped pitted kalamata or black olives
    1 tablespoon drained capers
   ¼ cup chopped fresh basil or parsley

1. Cook linguine according to package directions. Drain; set aside.

2. Meanwhile, heat oil in large nonstick skillet over medium high heat. Add shrimp, garlic and red pepper flakes; cook and stir 3 to 4 minutes or until shrimp are opaque. Transfer shrimp mixture to bowl with slotted spoon; set aside.

3. Add onion to same skillet; cook over medium heat 5 minutes, stirring occasionally. Add tomatoes with juice, tomato paste, olives and capers; simmer, uncovered, 5 minutes.

4. Return shrimp mixture to skillet; simmer 1 minute. Stir in basil; simmer 1 minute. Place linguine in large serving bowl; top with shrimp mixture.

Spicy Shrimp Puttanesca

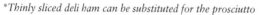

Spinach, Cheese and Prosciutto-Stuffed Chicken Breasts
Makes 4 servings

4 boneless skinless chicken breasts (about 4 ounces each)
  Salt and black pepper
4 slices (½ ounce each) prosciutto*
4 slices (½ ounce each) smoked provolone**
1 cup spinach leaves, chopped
4 tablespoons all-purpose flour, divided
1 tablespoon olive oil
1 tablespoon butter
1 cup chicken broth
1 tablespoon heavy cream

Thinly sliced deli ham can be substituted for the prosciutto

**Swiss, Gruyère or mozzarella cheese may be substituted for the smoked provolone*

1. Preheat oven to 350°F. To form pocket for stuffing, cut each chicken breast horizontally almost to opposite edge. Fold back top half of chicken breast; sprinkle chicken lightly with salt and pepper. Place 1 slice prosciutto, 1 slice provolone and ¼ cup spinach on each chicken breast. Fold top half of breasts over filling.

2. Spread 3 tablespoons flour on plate. Holding chicken breast closed, coat with flour; shake off excess. Lightly sprinkle chicken with salt and pepper.

3. Heat oil and butter in large skillet over medium heat. Place chicken in skillet; cook about 4 minutes on each side or until browned.

4. Transfer chicken to shallow baking dish. Bake 10 minutes or until chicken is no longer pink in center and juices run clear.

5. Whisk chicken broth and cream into remaining 1 tablespoon flour in small bowl. Pour chicken broth mixture into same skillet; heat over medium heat, stirring constantly, until sauce thickens, about 3 minutes. Spoon sauce onto serving plates; top with chicken breasts.

Tip: Prosciutto, an Italian ham, is seasoned, cured and air-dried, not smoked. Look for imported or less expensive domestic prosciutto in delis and Italian food markets.

Spinach, Cheese and Prosciutto-Stuffed Chicken Breast

135

Tuscan Pork with Peppers

Makes 4 servings

1 pound boneless pork chops, cut into 1-inch cubes
1 medium onion, peeled and chopped
2 cloves garlic, minced
1 teaspoon olive oil
1 (14½-ounce) can Italian-style tomatoes, undrained
½ cup dry white wine
1 sweet red bell pepper, seeded and sliced
1 green bell pepper, seeded and sliced

Sauté pork cubes, onion and garlic in olive oil in large nonstick skillet over medium-high heat until pork starts to brown, about 4 to 5 minutes. Add remaining ingredients; lower heat to a simmer. Cover and cook gently for 12 to 15 minutes. Taste for seasoning, adding salt and black pepper, if desired. Serve with hot cooked rigatoni or penne, if desired.

Prep Time: 30 minutes

Favorite recipe from **National Pork Board**

Tip: Green bell peppers are picked before they ripen. When ripe, a bell pepper is red, yellow, orange, white or purple, depending on the variety. They are sweeter and crisper than green peppers. Red peppers are generally more expensive because the yield is lower from each plant.

Chicken with Escarole and Eggplant

Makes 4 servings

4 bone-in chicken breast halves (about 1½ pounds)
2 tablespoons olive oil
1 tablespoon chopped garlic
1 large head escarole, chopped
1 small eggplant (about 1 pound), peeled and cubed
1 jar (1 pound 10 ounces) RAGÚ® Robusto! Pasta Sauce

1. Preheat oven to 450°F. Season chicken, if desired, with salt and pepper. In bottom of broiler pan without rack, arrange chicken. Roast 40 minutes or until chicken is thoroughly cooked in center.

2. Meanwhile, in 12-inch skillet, heat olive oil over medium heat and cook garlic, stirring occasionally, 30 seconds. Add escarole and eggplant and cook covered, stirring occasionally, 5 minutes, or until escarole is wilted. Stir in Ragú Robusto! Pasta Sauce and cook 10 minutes or until vegetables are tender.

3. With slotted spoon, remove vegetables to large serving platter, then top with chicken. Serve over hot cooked pasta or rice, if desired.

Prep Time: 10 minutes
Cook Time: 40 minutes

Stuffed Pork Loin Genoa Style

Makes 10 servings

1 (4- to 5-pound) boneless pork loin roast
1¼ cups chopped fresh parsley, divided
½ cup chopped fresh basil leaves
½ cup pine nuts
½ cup grated Parmesan cheese
6 cloves garlic, peeled and chopped
½ pound ground pork
½ pound Italian sausage
1 cup dry bread crumbs
¼ cup milk
1 egg
1 teaspoon ground black pepper

In food processor or blender, process 1 cup parsley, basil, pine nuts, Parmesan cheese and garlic. Set aside.

Mix together ground pork, Italian sausage, bread crumbs, milk, egg, remaining ¼ cup parsley and pepper.

Place roast fat-side down on cutting board. Spread with the herb-cheese mixture; place ground pork mixture along center of loin. Fold in half; tie with kitchen string. Roast on rack in shallow baking pan at 350°F for 1½ hours or until internal temperature reaches 155°F. Slice to serve.

Prep Time: 15 minutes
Cook Time: 90 minutes

Favorite recipe from **National Pork Board**

Stuffed Pork Loin Genoa Style

139

Swordfish Messina Style

Makes 8 servings

2 tablespoons olive or vegetable oil
½ cup chopped fresh parsley
2 tablespoons chopped fresh basil *or* 2 teaspoons dried basil leaves, crushed
2 cloves garlic, minced
1 can (8 ounces) CONTADINA® Tomato Sauce
¾ cup sliced fresh mushrooms
1 tablespoon capers
1 tablespoon lemon juice
⅛ teaspoon ground black pepper
3 pounds swordfish or halibut steaks

1. Heat oil in small saucepan. Add parsley, basil and garlic; sauté for 1 minute. Reduce heat to low. Add tomato sauce, mushrooms and capers; simmer, uncovered, for 5 minutes.

2. Stir in lemon juice and pepper. Place swordfish in single layer in greased 13×9-inch baking dish; cover with sauce.

3. Bake in preheated 400°F oven for 20 minutes or until fish flakes easily when tested with fork.

Prep Time: 5 minutes
Cook Time: 26 minutes

Swordfish Messina Style

Tuscan Chicken with White Beans

Makes 4 servings

1 large fresh fennel bulb (about ¾ pound)
1 tablespoon olive oil
8 ounces boneless skinless chicken thighs, cut into ¾-inch pieces
1 teaspoon dried rosemary leaves, crushed
½ teaspoon black pepper
1 can (14½ ounces) no-salt-added stewed tomatoes, undrained
1 can (14½ ounces) reduced-sodium chicken broth
1 can (about 15 ounces) cannellini beans, rinsed and drained
  Hot pepper sauce (optional)

1. Cut off and reserve ¼ cup chopped feathery fennel tops. Chop bulb into ½-inch pieces. Heat oil in large saucepan over medium heat. Add chopped fennel bulb; cook 5 minutes, stirring occasionally.

2. Sprinkle chicken with rosemary and pepper; add to saucepan. Cook and stir 2 minutes. Add tomatoes with juice and chicken broth; bring to a boil. Cover; simmer 10 minutes. Stir in beans; simmer, uncovered, 15 minutes or until chicken is cooked through and sauce thickens. Season to taste with hot pepper sauce, if desired. Ladle into 4 shallow bowls; top with reserved fennel tops.

Prep Time: 15 minutes
Cook Time: 35 minutes

Tip: Fennel has a crisp texture and a slightly sweet licoricelike flavor, which mellows when cooked.

Veal Scallopine

Classic Chicken Piccata
Makes 4 servings

4 boneless skinless chicken breast halves
¼ cup all-purpose flour
1 egg, beaten
½ cup bread crumbs
1 teaspoon dried parsley flakes
¼ teaspoon salt
¼ teaspoon pepper
3 tablespoons olive oil
⅓ cup dry white wine
¼ cup fresh lemon juice
Lemon slices for garnish (optional)

1. Place chicken between 2 pieces of plastic wrap; pound to ½-inch thickness. Place flour on small plate. Place egg in shallow bowl. Combine bread crumbs, parsley, salt and pepper on another small plate. Coat each breast half in flour, then in egg. Coat with bread crumb mixture.

2. Heat oil in medium nonstick skillet over medium-high heat. Add chicken; cook 4 minutes. Turn; reduce heat to medium. Cook 4 to 5 minutes or until chicken is no longer pink in center. Transfer chicken to serving platter; keep warm. Add wine and lemon juice to skillet; cook and stir over high heat 2 minutes. Spoon sauce over chicken. Garnish with lemon slices, if desired.

Tip: *A medium-size lemon will produce about 3 to 4 tablespoons of juice. Lemons will yield slightly more juice if they are brought to room temperature before squeezing.*

Classic Chicken Piccata

Light Meals

Caramelized Onion and Olive Pizza

Makes 8 to 10 servings

    2 tablespoons olive oil
1½ pounds onions, thinly sliced
    2 teaspoons fresh rosemary *or* 1 teaspoon dried rosemary leaves
    1 tablespoon balsamic vinegar
    1 cup California ripe olives, sliced
    1 (12-inch) prebaked thick pizza crust
    2 cups (8 ounces) shredded mozzarella cheese

Heat oil in medium nonstick skillet until hot. Add onions and rosemary. Cook, stirring frequently, until onions begin to brown and browned bits begin to stick to bottom of skillet, about 15 minutes. Stir in ¼ cup water; scrape up any browned bits. Reduce heat to medium-low and continue to cook, stirring occasionally, until onions are golden and sweet tasting, 15 to 30 minutes longer; add water, 1 tablespoon at a time, if pan appears dry. Remove pan from heat and stir in vinegar, scraping up any browned bits from pan. Gently stir in olives. Place crust on pizza pan or baking sheet. Spoon onion mixture into center of crust. Sprinkle with cheese. Bake in 450°F oven until cheese is melted and tinged with brown, about 15 minutes. Cut into wedges and serve warm.

Prep Time: 15 minutes
Cook Time: about 1 hour

Favorite recipe from **California Olive Industry**

Caramelized Onion and Olive Pizza

Artichoke Frittata

Makes 4 servings

1 can (14 ounces) artichoke hearts, drained
3 teaspoons olive oil, divided
½ cup minced green onions
5 eggs
½ cup (2 ounces) shredded Swiss cheese
2 tablespoons grated Parmesan cheese
1 tablespoon minced fresh parsley
1 teaspoon salt
  Black pepper

1. Chop artichoke hearts; set aside.

2. Heat 2 teaspoons oil in 10-inch skillet over medium heat. Add green onions; cook and stir until tender. Remove from skillet.

3. Beat eggs in medium bowl until light. Stir in artichokes, green onions, cheeses, parsley, salt and pepper to taste.

4. Heat remaining 1 teaspoon oil in same skillet over medium heat. Pour egg mixture into skillet. Cook 4 to 5 minutes or until bottom is lightly browned. Place large plate over skillet and invert frittata onto plate. Return frittata, uncooked side down, to skillet. Cook about 4 minutes more or until center is just set. Cut into wedges.

Tip: *A frittata is an Italian omelet in which the eggs are combined, before cooking, with other ingredients such as meat, vegetables and herbs. The egg mixture is poured into a heavy skillet and cooked slowly over low heat. This slow cooking produces a firmer egg dish than a traditional American omelet.*

Artichoke Frittata

Calzone Italiano

Makes 4 servings

Pizza dough for one 14-inch pizza
1 can (15 ounces) CONTADINA® Pizza Sauce, divided
3 ounces sliced pepperoni *or* ½ pound crumbled Italian sausage, cooked, drained
2 tablespoons chopped green bell pepper
1 cup (4 ounces) shredded mozzarella cheese
1 cup (8 ounces) ricotta cheese

1. Divide dough into 4 equal portions. Place on lightly floured large, rimless cookie sheet. Press or roll out dough to 7-inch circles.

2. Spread 2 tablespoons pizza sauce onto half of each circle to within ½ inch of edge; top with ¼ each pepperoni, bell pepper and mozzarella cheese.

3. Spoon ¼ cup ricotta cheese onto remaining half of each circle; fold dough over. Press edges together tightly to seal. Cut slits into top of dough to allow steam to escape.

4. Bake in preheated 350°F oven for 20 to 25 minutes or until crusts are golden brown. Meanwhile, heat remaining pizza sauce; serve over calzones.

Note: If desired, 1 large calzone may be made instead of 4 individual calzones. To prepare, shape dough into 1 (13-inch) circle. Spread ½ cup pizza sauce onto half of dough; proceed as above. Bake for 25 minutes.

Prep Time: 15 minutes
Cook Time: 25 minutes

Herbed Mushroom Pizza

Mediterranean Frittata

Makes 4 to 6 servings

¼ cup olive oil
5 small yellow onions, thinly sliced
1 can (14½ ounces) whole peeled tomatoes, drained and chopped
¼ pound prosciutto or cooked ham, chopped
¼ cup grated Parmesan cheese
2 tablespoons chopped fresh parsley
½ teaspoon dried marjoram leaves
¼ teaspoon dried basil leaves
¼ teaspoon salt
Generous dash black pepper
6 eggs
2 tablespoons butter or margarine
Italian parsley leaves for garnish (optional)

1. Heat oil in medium skillet over medium-high heat. Cook and stir onions in hot oil 6 to 8 minutes until soft and golden. Add tomatoes; cook and stir over medium heat 5 minutes. Remove tomatoes and onions to large bowl with slotted spoon; discard drippings. Cool tomato-onion mixture to room temperature.

2. Stir prosciutto, cheese, parsley, marjoram, basil, salt and pepper into cooled tomato-onion mixture. Whisk eggs in small bowl; stir into prosciutto mixture.

3. Preheat broiler. Heat butter in large broilerproof skillet over medium heat until melted and bubbly; reduce heat to low.

4. Add egg mixture to skillet, spreading evenly. Cook over low heat 8 to 10 minutes until all but top ¼ inch of egg mixture is set; shake pan gently to test. *Do not stir.*

5. Broil egg mixture about 4 inches from heat 1 to 2 minutes until top of egg mixture is set. (Do not brown or frittata will be dry.) Frittata can be served hot, at room temperature or cold. To serve, cut into wedges. Garnish, if desired.

Mediterranean Frittata

Pizza Romano

Makes 4 servings

1 (10-inch) prepared pizza crust *or* 4 rounds pita bread
1 cup (4 ounces) shredded mozzarella cheese
4 slices HILLSHIRE FARM® Ham, cut into ½-inch strips
1 jar (8 ounces) marinated sun-dried tomatoes, drained (optional)
1 jar (6 ounces) oil-packed artichokes, drained and cut into eighths
1 jar (4 ounces) roasted red peppers, drained and cut into strips

Preheat oven to 425°F.

Place pizza crust on cookie sheet; top with remaining ingredients. Bake on lower rack of oven 15 to 20 minutes or until crust begins to brown lightly and cheese is melted.

Leek Frittata

Makes 8 servings

3 leeks
4 eggs
1 large potato, cooked and mashed (about ½ cup)
½ cup grated Romano cheese
1 tablespoon FILIPPO BERIO® Olive Oil
½ teaspoon salt
½ teaspoon dried Italian herb seasoning

Preheat oven to 375°F. Grease bottom and side of 1-quart casserole dish or 8-inch round cake pan with olive oil. Cut off root ends and tops of leeks. Split leeks; wash thoroughly and drain. Thinly slice white and pale green parts to measure 2 cups. Steam leeks 8 to 10 minutes or until tender. In large bowl, beat eggs with electric mixer at medium speed until foamy. Stir in leeks, potato, Romano cheese, olive oil, salt and Italian seasoning. Pour into prepared dish. Bake 30 to 40 minutes or until top is golden brown.

BelGioioso® Caprese Sandwich

Makes 4 sandwiches

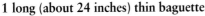

1 long (about 24 inches) thin baguette
1 clove garlic, cut in half
2 medium, fully-ripened tomatoes, thinly sliced and slices cut in half
24 fresh basil leaves
8 ounces BELGIOIOSO® Fresh Mozzarella, cut into ½-inch cubes
2 to 3 teaspoons extra virgin olive oil
2 teaspoons drained capers
    Salt and freshly ground black pepper to taste

Make lengthwise cut down middle of baguette, starting on top of loaf and cut into, but not through, bottom. Gently open to make V-shaped cavity.

Rub cut sides of bread with garlic. Arrange tomato slices down each side of cavity followed by basil leaves.

In medium bowl, gently mix BelGioioso Fresh Mozzarella, oil, capers, salt and pepper. Spoon mixture into loaf between rows of tomato and basil. Cut sandwich crosswise into 6-inch lengths.

Tip: Fresh mozzarella is usually packaged in water or whey. It has a much softer texture than regular mozzarella, with a sweet, delicate flavor.

Chicken Parmesan Stromboli

Makes 6 servings

1 pound boneless, skinless chicken breast halves
½ teaspoon salt
¼ teaspoon ground black pepper
2 teaspoons olive oil
2 cups shredded mozzarella cheese (about 8 ounces)
1 jar (1 pound 10 ounces) RAGÚ® Chunky Gardenstyle Pasta Sauce, divided
2 tablespoons grated Parmesan cheese
1 tablespoon finely chopped fresh parsley
1 pound fresh or thawed frozen bread dough

1. Preheat oven to 400°F. Season chicken with salt and pepper. In 12-inch skillet, heat olive oil over medium-high heat and brown chicken. Remove chicken from skillet and let cool; pull into large shreds.

2. In medium bowl, combine chicken, mozzarella cheese, ½ cup Ragú Chunky Gardenstyle Pasta Sauce, Parmesan cheese and parsley; set aside.

3. On greased jelly-roll pan, press dough to form 12×10-inch rectangle. Arrange chicken mixture down center of dough. Cover filling by bringing one long side of dough into center, then overlap with the other long side; pinch seam to seal. Fold in ends and pinch to seal. Arrange on pan, seam-side down. Gently press in sides to form 12×4-inch loaf. Bake 35 minutes or until dough is cooked and golden. Cut stromboli into slices. Heat remaining pasta sauce and serve with stromboli.

Chicken Parmesan Stromboli

Sausage, Peppers & Onion Pizza
Makes 8 servings

½ pound bulk Italian sausage
1 medium red bell pepper, cut into strips
1 pre-baked pizza crust (14 inches)
1 cup spaghetti or pizza sauce
1½ cups shredded mozzarella cheese
1⅓ cups *French's*® French Fried Onions

1. Preheat oven to 450°F. Cook sausage in nonstick skillet over medium heat until browned, stirring frequently; drain. Add bell pepper and cook until crisp-tender, stirring occasionally.

2. Top pizza crust with sauce, sausage mixture and cheese. Bake 8 to 10 minutes or until cheese melts. Sprinkle with French Fried Onions; bake 2 minutes or until onions are golden.

Tip: You may substitute link sausage; remove meat from casing.

Prep Time: 10 minutes
Cook Time: 17 minutes

Tip: Kitchen scissors are a great tool for cutting pizza—neater and easier to handle than a pizza cutter.

Sausage, Peppers & Onion Pizza

Linguine Frittata

Makes 6 to 8 servings

8 ounces uncooked linguine
3 tablespoons olive oil, divided
1 cup chopped carrots
¼ cup chopped onion
2 cloves garlic, minced
½ pound asparagus, cut into 1-inch pieces
1 large red bell pepper, diced
1 medium tomato, seeded and chopped
1 teaspoon dried basil leaves
1 teaspoon dried marjoram leaves
1 teaspoon dried oregano leaves
5 eggs, beaten
¼ cup grated Parmesan cheese
½ teaspoon salt
¼ teaspoon black pepper

1. Cook linguine according to package directions. Drain in colander. Place in large bowl.

2. Heat 1 tablespoon oil in large skillet over medium heat until hot. Add carrots, onion and garlic; cook and stir 5 minutes or until carrots are crisp-tender. Add asparagus, bell pepper, tomato, basil, marjoram and oregano; cook and stir 5 minutes or until asparagus is crisp-tender. Add vegetable mixture to linguine in bowl; mix well.

3. Beat eggs in medium bowl with wire whisk until frothy. Stir in cheese, salt and black pepper; pour over linguine mixture and toss.

4. Heat remaining 2 tablespoons oil in 12-inch nonstick skillet over medium heat until hot. Add linguine mixture, spreading evenly. Reduce heat to low. Cook 5 minutes or until browned on bottom. Place large rimless plate over skillet; invert frittata onto plate. Slide frittata back into skillet. Cook 5 minutes more or until browned on bottom and eggs are set. Slide frittata onto serving plate. Cut into wedges.

Linguine Frittata

Quattro Formaggio Pizza
Makes 4 servings

1 (12-inch) Italian bread shell
½ cup prepared pizza or marinara sauce
4 ounces shaved or thinly sliced provolone cheese
1 cup (4 ounces) shredded smoked or regular mozzarella cheese
2 ounces Asiago or brick cheese, thinly sliced
¼ cup freshly grated Parmesan or Romano cheese

1. Preheat oven to 450°F.

2. Place bread shell on baking sheet. Spread pizza sauce evenly over bread shell. Top with provolone, mozzarella, Asiago and Parmesan cheeses.

3. Bake 14 minutes or until bread shell is golden brown and cheese is melted. Cut into wedges; serve immediately.

Tip: Quattro Formaggio is Italian for "four cheeses." This pizza is a snap to prepare and is sure to please all the cheese lovers in your family.

Quattro Formaggio Pizza

171

Tuscan-Style Sausage Sandwiches

Makes 4 servings

1 pound hot or sweet Italian sausage links, sliced
1 box (10 ounces) frozen chopped spinach, thawed and squeezed dry
1 small onion, sliced
½ cup fresh or drained canned sliced mushrooms
1 jar (1 pound 10 ounces) RAGÚ® Robusto! Pasta Sauce
1 loaf Italian or French bread (about 16 inches long), cut into 4 rolls

In 12-inch skillet, brown sausage over medium-high heat. Stir in spinach, onion and mushrooms. Cook, stirring occasionally, 5 minutes or until sausage is cooked through. Stir in Ragú Robusto! Pasta Sauce; heat through.

For each sandwich, split open each roll and evenly spoon in sausage mixture. Sprinkle with crushed red pepper flakes, if desired.

Grilled Panini Sandwiches

Makes 4 servings

8 slices country Italian, sourdough or other firm-textured bread
8 slices SARGENTO® Deli Style Sliced Mozzarella Cheese
⅓ cup prepared pesto
4 large slices ripe tomato
2 tablespoons olive oil

1. Top each of 4 slices of bread with a slice of cheese. Spread pesto over cheese. Arrange tomatoes on top, then another slice of cheese. Close sandwiches with remaining 4 slices bread.

2. Brush olive oil lightly over both sides of sandwiches. Cook sandwiches over medium-low coals or in a preheated ridged grill pan over medium heat 3 to 4 minutes per side or until bread is toasted and cheese is melted.

Prep Time: 5 minutes
Cook Time: 8 minutes

Tuscan-Style Sausage Sandwich

Panini with Prosciutto, Mozzarella and Ripe Olives

Makes 8 servings

  1 cup California ripe olives, sliced
¼ cup chopped fresh basil
  8 wedges prepared herbed focaccia
⅓ cup coarse mustard
  1 pound prosciutto, sliced
24 ounces mozzarella, thinly sliced
  4 cups arugula, washed, dried

Combine sliced olives and basil in bowl. Mix well and reserve. Slice each focaccia wedge in half. Spread cut sides of each wedge with 1 teaspoon mustard. Layer bottom halves with 2 tablespoons olive mixture, 2 ounces prosciutto, 3 ounces mozzarella and ½ cup arugula. Top with remaining focaccia halves.

Favorite recipe from **California Olive Industry**

BelGioioso® Mozzarella Pizza

Makes 2 pizzas

  2 (13-inch) refrigerated pizza crusts
  3 tablespoons olive oil, divided
  4 ripe plum tomatoes, cut into thin slices
  2 cups diced BELGIOIOSO® Fresh Mozzarella Cheese
12 fresh basil leaves
½ teaspoon salt

Preheat oven to 425°F. Place pizza crusts on lightly oiled pans. Brush each with 1 tablespoon olive oil. Place tomato slices on crusts; layer with BelGioioso Fresh Mozzarella Cheese and basil leaves. Sprinkle with salt and remaining 1 tablespoon olive oil. Bake pizzas 25 to 30 minutes or until top and bottom of crusts are nicely browned. Cut into wedges and serve.

Stromboli

Makes 12 servings

1 package (10 ounces) refrigerated pizza dough
⅓ cup *French's*® Bold n' Spicy Brown Mustard
¾ pound sliced deli meats and cheese such as salami, provolone cheese and ham
1 egg, beaten
1 teaspoon poppy or sesame seeds

1. Preheat oven to 425°F. Unroll pizza dough on lightly floured board. Roll into 13×10-inch rectangle. Spread mustard evenly on dough. Layer luncheon meats and cheeses on dough, overlapping slices, leaving a 1-inch border around edges.

2. Fold one-third of dough toward center from long edge of rectangle. Fold second side toward center enclosing filling. Pinch long edge to seal. Pinch ends together and tuck under dough. Place on greased baking sheet.

3. Cut shallow crosswise slits on top of dough, spacing 3 inches apart. Brush stromboli lightly with beaten egg; sprinkle with poppy seeds. Bake 15 to 18 minutes or until deep golden brown. Remove to rack; cool slightly. Serve warm.

Prep Time: 20 minutes
Cook Time: 15 minutes

Onion and Pepper Calzones

Makes 10 small calzones

  1 tablespoon olive oil
  ½ cup chopped onion
  ½ cup chopped green bell pepper
  ¼ teaspoon salt
  ⅛ teaspoon dried basil leaves
  ⅛ teaspoon dried oregano leaves
  ⅛ teaspoon black pepper
  1 can (12 ounces) country biscuits (10 biscuits)
  ¼ cup (1 ounce) shredded mozzarella cheese
  ½ cup prepared spaghetti or pizza sauce
  2 tablespoons grated Parmesan cheese

1. Preheat oven to 400°F. Heat oil in medium nonstick skillet over medium-high heat. Add onion and bell pepper; cook 5 minutes, stirring occasionally. Remove from heat. Add salt, basil, oregano and black pepper; stir to combine. Cool slightly.

2. While onion mixture is cooling, flatten biscuits into 3½-inch circles about ⅛ inch thick using palm of hand.

3. Stir mozzarella cheese into onion mixture; spoon 1 teaspoonful onto each biscuit. Fold biscuits in half, covering filling. Press edges with tines of fork to seal; transfer to baking sheet.

4. Bake 10 to 12 minutes or until golden brown. While calzones are baking, place spaghetti sauce in small microwavable bowl. Cover with vented plastic wrap. Microwave at HIGH 3 minutes or until hot.

5. To serve, spoon spaghetti sauce and Parmesan cheese evenly over each calzone. Serve immediately.

Onion and Pepper Calzones

Roma Tomato Pizzas

Makes 2 (15-inch) pizzas

  2 loaves (1 pound each) frozen bread dough, thawed
 ⅓ cup olive oil
  2 cups thinly sliced onions
  2 cloves garlic, minced
 12 Roma (Italian plum) tomatoes, sliced ⅛-inch thick
  1 teaspoon dried basil leaves
  1 teaspoon dried oregano leaves
    Black pepper
  1 cup grated Parmesan cheese
  1 can (2¼ ounces) sliced, pitted ripe olives, drained
    Green and yellow bell pepper strips

1. Preheat oven to 450°F. Roll out each loaf on lightly floured surface into 15-inch circle; press each into greased 15-inch pizza pan or stretch into 15×10-inch baking pan. Crimp edges to form rim; prick several times with fork. Bake crusts 10 minutes. Remove from oven; set aside.

2. Reduce oven temperature to 400°F. Heat oil in large skillet over medium-high heat until hot. Add onions and garlic; cook and stir 6 to 8 minutes or until onions are tender. Divide onion mixture (including olive oil) between crusts. Arrange tomato slices evenly over onion mixture. Sprinkle each pizza with ½ teaspoon basil leaves, ½ teaspoon oregano leaves and black pepper to taste. Sprinkle each pizza with ½ cup Parmesan cheese. Top with olives and desired amount of bell peppers. Bake 10 to 15 minutes or until toppings are heated through.

Roma Tomato Pizza

Side Dishes

Pepperoni-Oregano Focaccia
Makes 12 servings

 1 tablespoon cornmeal
 1 package (10 ounces) refrigerated pizza crust dough
 ½ cup finely chopped pepperoni (3 to 3½ ounces)
 1½ teaspoons finely chopped fresh oregano *or* ½ teaspoon dried oregano leaves
 2 teaspoons olive oil

1. Preheat oven to 425°F. Grease large baking sheet; sprinkle with cornmeal.

2. Unroll dough onto lightly floured surface. Pat dough into 12×9-inch rectangle. Sprinkle half the pepperoni and half the oregano over one side of dough. Fold over dough to make 12×4½-inch rectangle.

3. Roll dough into 12×9-inch rectangle. Place on prepared baking sheet. Prick dough with fork at 2-inch intervals about 30 times. Brush with oil; sprinkle with remaining pepperoni and oregano.

4. Bake 12 to 15 minutes until golden brown. (Prick dough several more times if dough puffs as it bakes.) Cut into strips.

Pepperoni-Oregano Focaccia

Zucchini-Tomato Bake
Makes 6 servings

1 pound eggplant, coarsely chopped
2 cups zucchini slices
2 cups mushroom slices
3 sheets (18×12 inches) heavy-duty foil, lightly sprayed with nonstick
    cooking spray
2 teaspoons olive oil
½ cup chopped onion
½ cup chopped fresh fennel (optional)
2 cloves garlic, minced
1 can (14½ ounces) no-salt-added whole tomatoes, undrained
1 tablespoon no-salt-added tomato paste
2 teaspoons dried basil leaves
1 teaspoon sugar

1. Preheat oven to 400°F. Divide eggplant, zucchini and mushrooms into
3 portions. Arrange each portion on foil sheet.

2. Heat oil in small skillet over medium heat. Add onion, fennel, if desired,
and garlic. Cook and stir 3 to 4 minutes or until onion is tender. Add
tomatoes with juice, tomato paste, basil and sugar. Cook and stir about
4 minutes or until sauce thickens.

3. Pour sauce over eggplant mixture. Double-fold sides and ends of foil to
seal packets, leaving head space for heat circulation. Place on baking sheet.

4. Bake 30 minutes. Remove from oven. Carefully open one end of each
packet to allow steam to escape. Open and transfer contents to serving dish.
Garnish, if desired.

Zucchini-Tomato Bake

Lemon and Fennel Marinated Vegetables

Makes 4 servings

1 cup water
2 medium carrots, cut diagonally into ½-inch-thick slices
1 cup small whole fresh mushrooms
1 small red or green bell pepper, cut into ¾-inch pieces
3 tablespoons lemon juice
1 tablespoon sugar
1 tablespoon olive oil
1 clove garlic, minced
½ teaspoon fennel seeds, crushed
½ teaspoon dried basil leaves, crushed
¼ teaspoon black pepper

1. Bring water to a boil in small saucepan over high heat. Add carrots; return to a boil. Reduce heat to medium-low. Cover and simmer about 5 minutes or until carrots are crisp-tender. Drain and cool.

2. Place carrots, mushrooms and bell pepper in large resealable plastic food storage bag. Combine lemon juice, sugar, oil, garlic, fennel seeds, basil and black pepper in small bowl. Pour over vegetables. Close bag securely; turn to coat. Marinate in refrigerator 8 to 24 hours, turning occasionally.

3. Drain vegetables; discard marinade. Transfer vegetables to serving dish.

Tip: *To clean mushrooms, wipe them with a damp paper towel, brush with a mushroom brush, or rinse briefly under cold running water to remove the dirt. Pat dry before using. Never soak them in water because they absorb water and will become mushy.*

Lemon and Fennel Marinated Vegetables

Vegetables Italiano

Makes 4 side-dish servings

    2 tablespoons olive oil
    1 cup sliced peeled carrots
    ¾ cup halved onion slices
    2 cloves garlic, minced
    1 can (14.5 ounces) CONTADINA® Stewed Tomatoes, undrained
    3 cups sliced zucchini
    1 cup fresh mushrooms, halved
    ¼ teaspoon salt, or to taste
    ⅛ teaspoon ground black pepper

1. Heat oil in large skillet. Add carrots, onion and garlic; sauté for 3 minutes.

2. Stir in undrained tomatoes, zucchini, mushrooms, salt and pepper.

3. Bring to a boil. Reduce heat to low; simmer, uncovered, for 5 to 6 minutes or until vegetables are crisp-tender. Serve over pasta, if desired.

Prep Time: 8 minutes
Cook Time: 10 minutes

Artichoke Hearts Marinara

Makes 4 side-dish servings

1 pound baby artichokes (about 12)
1 lemon half
2 tablespoons olive oil
½ cup chopped onion
1 clove garlic, minced
½ cup chicken broth
1 cup prepared marinara or spaghetti sauce
¼ cup freshly grated Parmesan cheese
   Lemon wedges and artichoke leaves for garnish (optional)

1. Rinse artichokes under running water. Bend back outer green leaves and snap off at base. Continue snapping off leaves until top halves of leaves are green and bottom halves are yellow.

2. Cut off green fibrous tops of leaves, parallel to base; discard tips. Cut stems off, level with base. Cut in half lengthwise (from top). To help prevent discoloration, rub ends with lemon.

3. Heat oil in large skillet over medium-high heat. Cook and stir artichoke hearts, onion and garlic in hot oil 5 to 10 minutes until onion is soft and golden. Add broth; cover. Bring to a boil over high heat; reduce heat to medium-low. Simmer 10 to 15 minutes. Uncover and boil until liquid has evaporated.

4. Preheat broiler. Spread marinara sauce in bottom of 8-inch square broilerproof baking dish or 4 individual broilerproof serving dishes. Arrange artichoke hearts cut side down in sauce. Sprinkle with cheese. Brown under broiler about 5 minutes or until sauce is heated through and cheese is melted. Garnish, if desired. Serve immediately.

Sesame Italian Breadsticks

Makes 12 breadsticks

¼ cup grated Parmesan cheese
3 tablespoons sesame seeds
2 teaspoons Italian seasoning
1 teaspoon kosher salt (optional)
12 frozen bread dough dinner rolls, thawed
¼ cup butter, melted

1. Preheat oven to 425°F. Spray large baking sheet with nonstick cooking spray.

2. Combine Parmesan cheese, sesame seeds, Italian seasoning and salt, if desired; spread out on plate.

3. Roll each dinner roll into rope, about 8 inches long and ½ inch thick, on lightly floured surface. Place on baking sheet; brush tops and sides with butter. Roll each buttered rope in cheese mixture, pressing mixture into dough. Return ropes to baking sheet, placing 2 inches apart. Twist each rope 3 times, pressing both ends of rope down on baking sheet. Bake 10 to 12 minutes or until golden brown.

Sesame Italian Breadsticks

189

Cannellini Parmesan Casserole

Makes 6 servings

2 tablespoons olive oil
1 cup chopped onion
2 teaspoons minced garlic
1 teaspoon dried oregano leaves
¼ teaspoon black pepper
2 cans (14½ ounces each) diced tomatoes with onion and garlic, undrained
1 jar (14 ounces) roasted red peppers, drained and cut into ½-inch pieces
2 cans (19 ounces each) white cannellini beans or Great Northern beans, rinsed and drained
1 teaspoon dried basil leaves *or* 1 tablespoon chopped fresh basil
¾ cup grated Parmesan cheese

1. Heat oil in Dutch oven over medium heat until hot. Add onion, garlic, oregano and pepper; cook and stir 5 minutes or until onion is tender.

2. Increase heat to high. Add tomatoes with juice and red peppers; cover and bring to a boil.

3. Reduce heat to medium. Stir in beans; cover and simmer 5 minutes, stirring occasionally. Stir in basil and sprinkle with cheese.

Cannellini Parmesan Casserole

Creamy Spinach Italiano

Makes 4 servings

    1 cup ricotta cheese
 ¾ cup half-and-half or milk
    2 packages (10 ounces each) frozen chopped spinach, thawed and squeezed dry
1⅓ cups *French's®* French Fried Onions, divided
 ½ cup chopped roasted red pepper
 ¼ cup chopped fresh basil
 ¼ cup grated Parmesan cheese
    1 teaspoon garlic powder
 ¼ teaspoon salt

1. Preheat oven to 350°F. Whisk together ricotta cheese and half-and-half in large bowl until well combined. Stir in spinach, ⅔ *cup* French Fried Onions, red pepper, basil, Parmesan, garlic powder and salt. Pour mixture into greased deep-dish 9-inch pie plate.

2. Bake for 25 minutes or until heated through; stir. Sprinkle with remaining ⅔ *cup* onions. Bake for 5 minutes or until onions are golden.

Peas Florentine Style

Makes 5 servings

    2 (10-ounce) packages frozen peas
 ¼ cup FILIPPO BERIO® Olive Oil
    4 ounces Canadian bacon, cubed
    1 clove garlic, minced
    1 tablespoon chopped fresh Italian parsley
    1 teaspoon sugar
       Salt

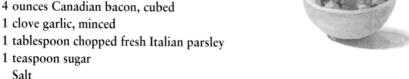

Place peas in large colander or strainer; run under hot water until slightly thawed. Drain well. In medium skillet, heat olive oil over medium heat until hot. Add bacon and garlic; cook and stir 2 to 3 minutes or until garlic turns golden. Add peas and parsley; cook and stir over high heat 5 to 7 minutes or until heated through. Drain well. Stir in sugar; season to taste with salt.

Creamy Spinach Italiano

Fennel with Parmesan Bread Crumbs

Makes 4 servings

2 large fennel bulbs
½ cup dry bread crumbs
¼ cup lemon juice
1 tablespoon freshly grated Parmesan cheese
1 tablespoon capers
2 teaspoons olive oil
⅛ teaspoon black pepper
½ cup reduced-sodium chicken broth
  Minced fennel leaves and red bell pepper strips for garnish (optional)

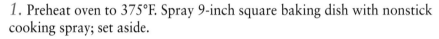

1. Preheat oven to 375°F. Spray 9-inch square baking dish with nonstick cooking spray; set aside.

2. Remove outer leaves and wide base from fennel bulbs. Slice bulbs crosswise.

3. Combine fennel and ¼ cup water in medium nonstick skillet with tight-fitting lid. Bring to a boil over high heat; reduce heat to medium. Cover; steam 4 minutes or until fennel is crisp-tender. Cool slightly; arrange in prepared baking pan.

4. Combine bread crumbs, lemon juice, Parmesan cheese, capers, oil and black pepper in small bowl. Sprinkle bread crumb mixture over fennel; pour broth over top.

5. Bake, uncovered, 20 to 25 minutes or until golden brown. Garnish, if desired.

Tip: Capers are deep green flower buds of a Mediterranean bush that have been preserved in a vinegary brine; they add pungency to sauces, dips and relishes. They should be rinsed in cold water to remove excess salt before using.

Fennel with Parmesan Bread Crumbs

Oven-Roasted Peppers and Onions

Makes 6 servings

　Nonstick olive oil cooking spray
2 medium green bell peppers
2 medium red bell peppers
2 medium yellow bell peppers
4 small onions
1 teaspoon dried Italian seasoning
½ teaspoon dried basil leaves
¼ teaspoon ground cumin

1. Preheat oven to 375°F. Spray 15×10-inch jelly-roll pan with cooking spray. Cut bell peppers into 1½-inch pieces. Cut onions into quarters. Place vegetables on prepared pan. Spray vegetables with cooking spray. Bake 20 minutes; stir. Sprinkle with Italian seasoning, basil and cumin.

2. Increase oven temperature to 425°F. Bake 20 minutes or until vegetables are crisp-tender and edges are lightly browned.

Herbed Green Beans

Makes 6 servings

1 pound fresh green beans, ends removed
1 teaspoon extra-virgin olive oil
2 tablespoons chopped fresh basil *or* 2 teaspoons dried basil leaves

1. Steam green beans 5 minutes or until crisp-tender. Rinse under cold running water; drain and set aside.

2. Just before serving, heat oil in large nonstick skillet over medium-low heat. Add basil; cook and stir 1 minute. Add green beans; cook until heated through. Garnish with additional fresh basil, if desired. Serve immediately.

Tip: When buying green beans, look for vivid green, crisp beans without scars. Pods should be well shaped and slim with small seeds. Buy beans of uniform size to ensure even cooking and avoid bruised or large beans.

Oven-Roasted Peppers and Onions

Broccoli Italian Style

Makes 4 servings

1¼ pounds broccoli
2 tablespoons lemon juice
1 teaspoon olive oil
1 clove garlic, minced
1 teaspoon chopped fresh parsley
Dash pepper

1. Trim broccoli, discarding tough part of stems. Cut broccoli into florets with 2-inch stems. Peel remaining broccoli stems; cut into ½-inch-thick slices.

2. Bring 1 quart water to a boil in large saucepan over high heat. Add broccoli; return to a boil. Reduce heat to medium-high. Cook, uncovered, 3 to 5 minutes or until broccoli is fork-tender. Drain; arrange in serving dish.

3. Combine lemon juice, oil, garlic, parsley and pepper in small bowl. Pour over broccoli, turning to coat. Let stand, covered, 1 to 2 hours before serving to allow flavors to blend.

Tip: Choose firm broccoli stems with tightly packed dark green buds and crisp leaves. Avoid bunches with wilted, yellowed leaves, open buds or tiny yellow flowers which indicate overmaturity.

Classica™ *Fontina Potato Surprise*

Makes about 8 servings

2½ pounds potatoes
3 tablespoons butter or margarine, melted
¼ cup CLASSICA™ Grated Parmesan cheese
1 egg
1 egg white
⅛ teaspoon salt
⅛ teaspoon ground nutmeg
4 tablespoons fine dry bread crumbs, divided
8 ounces fontina, cut into chunks
¼ cup freshly grated sharp provolone cheese
¼ pound GALBANI® Prosciutto di Parma, cut into small pieces
2 tablespoons butter or margarine, cut into small pieces

In large saucepan, cook potatoes in boiling water over medium-low heat until tender; drain. Cool slightly; peel and cut in half. Press potatoes through food mill or mash until smooth. Combine potatoes, melted butter, Classica™ Grated Parmesan Cheese, egg, egg white, salt and nutmeg in large bowl; mix until smooth. Set aside.

Sprinkle ½ of bread crumbs in well-buttered 9-inch round baking dish. Tilt dish to coat. Spread about ½ of potato mixture on bottom and side of dish.

Combine fontina, provolone and Galbani® Prosciutto di Parma in small bowl. Sprinkle over potato mixture in dish.

Cover with remaining potato mixture; sprinkle with remaining bread crumbs. Dot with pieces of butter.

Bake in preheated 350°F oven 40 minutes or until thin crust forms. Let stand 5 minutes.

Invert baking dish onto serving plate, tapping gently to remove. Serve immediately.

Desserts

Italian Ice

Makes 4 servings

1 cup sugar
1 cup water
1 cup sweet or dry fruity white wine
1 cup lemon juice
2 egg whites*
  Fresh berries
  Mint leaves for garnish (optional)

Use clean, uncracked grade A eggs.

1. Combine sugar, water and wine in small saucepan. Cook over medium-high heat until sugar has dissolved and syrup boils, stirring frequently. Cover; boil 1 minute. Uncover; adjust heat to maintain simmer. Simmer 10 minutes without stirring. Remove from heat. Refrigerate 1 hour or until syrup is completely cool.

2. Stir lemon juice into cooled syrup. Pour into 9-inch round cake pan. Freeze 1 hour.

3. Quickly stir mixture with fork breaking up ice crystals. Freeze 1 hour more or until firm but not solid. Meanwhile, place medium bowl in freezer to chill.

4. Beat egg whites in small bowl with electric mixer at high speed until stiff peaks form. Remove lemon ice mixture from cake pan to chilled bowl. Immediately beat ice with whisk or fork until smooth. Fold in egg whites; mix well. Spread egg white mixture evenly into same cake pan. Freeze 30 minutes. Immediately stir with fork; cover cake pan with foil. Freeze at least 3 hours or until firm.

5. To serve, scoop ice into fluted champagne glasses or dessert dishes. Serve with berries. Garnish, if desired.

Italian Ice

Chocolate Almond Biscotti
Makes about 2½ dozen cookies

½ cup (1 stick) butter or margarine, softened
1¼ cups sugar
2 eggs
1 teaspoon almond extract
2¼ cups all-purpose flour
¼ cup HERSHEY'S Dutch Processed Cocoa or HERSHEY'S Cocoa
1 teaspoon baking powder
¼ teaspoon salt
1 cup sliced almonds
Chocolate Glaze and White Glaze (recipes follow)
Additional sliced almonds (optional)

1. Heat oven to 350°F. Beat butter and sugar until blended. Add eggs and almond extract; beat well. Stir together flour, cocoa, baking powder and salt; gradually add to butter mixture, beating until smooth. (Dough will be thick.) Stir in almonds using wooden spoon.

2. Shape dough into two 11-inch-long rolls. Place rolls 3 to 4 inches apart on large ungreased cookie sheet.

3. Bake 30 minutes or until rolls are set. Remove from oven; cool on cookie sheet 15 minutes. Using serrated knife, cut rolls diagonally using sawing motion into ½-inch-thick slices. Arrange slices, cut sides down, close together on cookie sheet.

4. Bake 8 to 9 minutes. Turn slices over; bake 8 to 9 minutes more. Remove from oven; cool on cookie sheet on wire rack. Prepare Chocolate Glaze. Dip end of each biscotti in glaze or drizzle over entire cookie. Prepare White Glaze; drizzle over chocolate glaze. Garnish with additional almonds, if desired.

Chocolate Glaze: Place 1 cup HERSHEY'S Semi-Sweet Chocolate Chips and 1 tablespoon shortening (do not use butter, margarine, spread or oil) into small microwave-safe bowl. Microwave at HIGH (100%) 1 to 1½ minutes or until smooth when stirred. Makes about 1 cup glaze.

White Glaze: Place ¼ cup HERSHEY'S Premier White Chips and 1 teaspoon shortening (do not use butter, margarine, spread or oil) into small microwave-safe bowl. Microwave at HIGH (100%) 30 to 45 seconds or until smooth when stirred. Makes about ¼ cup glaze.

Chocolate Almond Biscotti

Strawberry Tiramisu
Makes 4 to 6 servings

16 ounces BELGIOIOSO® Mascarpone, at room temperature
¾ cup powdered sugar
7 tablespoons Marsala, divided
1 pint strawberries
¾ cup boiling water
2 tablespoons granulated sugar
2½ teaspoons instant espresso powder or instant coffee powder
1 (3.5-ounce) package Champagne biscuits (ladyfinger-style cookies)
1 ounce bittersweet or semi-sweet chocolate, grated

Blend BelGioioso Mascarpone, powdered sugar and 5 tablespoons Marsala in food processor until smooth. Slice half of strawberries; cut all remaining strawberries in half.

Combine boiling water, granulated sugar and espresso powder in medium bowl; stir to dissolve. Stir in remaining 2 tablespoons Marsala. Dip 1 Champagne biscuit briefly into espresso mixture, turning to coat. Place flat side up in bottom of 8-inch square glass baking dish with 2-inch-high sides. Repeat with enough biscuits to cover bottom of baking dish.

Spread ⅔ of mascarpone mixture over biscuits. Cover with sliced strawberries. Dip additional biscuits into espresso mixture and arrange over sliced strawberries, covering completely and trimming to fit. Spread remaining mascarpone mixture over biscuits. Sprinkle with grated chocolate. Arrange halved strawberries around edge of dish. Cover and refrigerate until set, at least 4 hours. (Tiramisu can be prepared 1 day ahead.) Cut into squares and serve.

Italian Chocolate Pie alla Lucia
Makes 8 servings

¼ cup pine nuts
3 tablespoons packed brown sugar
1 tablespoon grated orange peel
1 unbaked (9-inch) pie crust
4 ounces bittersweet chocolate, coarsely chopped
3 tablespoons unsalted butter
1 can (5 ounces) evaporated milk
3 eggs
3 tablespoons hazelnut liqueur
1 teaspoon vanilla
  Whipped cream (optional)
  Chocolate curls (optional)

1. Toast pine nuts in dry nonstick skillet over medium heat, stirring constantly until golden brown. Remove from heat and finely chop; cool. Combine pine nuts, brown sugar and orange peel in small bowl. Sprinkle onto bottom of pie crust; gently press into crust with fingertips or back of spoon.

2. Preheat oven to 325°F. Melt chocolate and butter in small saucepan over low heat; stir until blended and smooth. Let cool to room temperature.

3. Beat chocolate mixture and evaporated milk in medium bowl with electric mixer at medium speed. Add eggs, one at a time, beating well after each addition. Stir in hazelnut liqueur and vanilla. Pour into pie crust.

4. Bake on center rack of oven 30 to 40 minutes or until filling is set. Cool completely on wire rack. Refrigerate until ready to serve. Serve with whipped cream and chocolate curls, if desired.

Tip: To make chocolate curls, melt ½ cup semisweet chocolate chips and 1 teaspoon vegetable oil in a medium microwavable bowl on MEDIUM (50% power) 1 minute. Spread the chocolate mixture into 2-inch-wide ribbons on parchment paper. Let set 1 minute; then use the edge of a spatula to scrape the chocolate into curls. Place curls on a parchment paper-lined baking sheet. Let stand until set or refrigerate until ready to use.

Polenta Apricot Pudding Cake

Makes 8 servings

¼ cup chopped dried apricots
2 cups orange juice
1 cup part-skim ricotta cheese
3 tablespoons honey
¾ cup sugar
½ cup all-purpose flour
½ cup cornmeal
¼ teaspoon grated nutmeg
¼ cup slivered almonds
   Powdered sugar (optional)

1. Preheat oven to 300°F. Spray 10-inch nonstick springform pan with nonstick cooking spray. Soak apricots in ¼ cup water in small bowl 15 minutes. Drain and discard water. Pat apricots dry with paper towels.

2. Combine orange juice, ricotta cheese and honey in medium bowl. Beat at medium speed of electric mixer 5 minutes or until smooth. Combine sugar, flour, cornmeal and nutmeg in small bowl. Gradually add sugar mixture to orange juice mixture; blend well. Slowly stir in apricots.

3. Pour batter into prepared pan. Sprinkle with almonds. Bake 60 to 70 minutes or until center is firm and cake is golden brown. Garnish with powdered sugar, if desired. Serve warm.

Tip: Whenever possible, use freshly grated nutmeg in cooking and baking recipes. It's very quick and easy to grate nutmeg with a small, inexpensive hand grater, and freshly grated nutmeg has much more flavor than pre-packaged ground nutmeg.

Polenta Apricot Pudding Cake

Macédoine
Makes 8 servings

Finely grated peel and juice of 1 lemon
Finely grated peel and juice of 1 lime
8 cups diced assorted seasonal fruits*
1 cup sweet spumante wine or freshly squeezed orange juice
¼ cup sugar
¼ cup coarsely chopped walnuts or almonds, toasted (optional)

Apples, pears and bananas are essential fruits in a traditional Macédoine. Add as many seasonally ripe fruits to them as you can—variety is the key. As you select fruits, try to achieve a diversity of textures, being sure to avoid mushy, overripe fruit.

1. Combine lemon juice and lime juice; place in large bowl. Place assorted fruits in bowl with citrus juice mixture; toss to coat.

2. Combine wine, sugar and citrus peels in small bowl, stirring until sugar is dissolved. Pour over fruit mixture; toss gently. Cover; refrigerate 1 hour.

3. Sprinkle walnuts on fruit mixture just before serving, if desired.

Tip: Spumante is the Italian word for "sparkling." Asti Spumante is a sweet sparkling wine from Northern Italy which is often served as a dessert wine and occasionally as an apéritif.

Macédoine

Tiramisu

Makes 8 servings

2 tablespoons instant coffee crystals
½ cup hot water
2 (3-ounce) packages ladyfingers (24), cut crosswise into quarters
1 (14-ounce) can EAGLE BRAND® Sweetened Condensed Milk
    (NOT evaporated milk), divided
8 ounces mascarpone or cream cheese, softened
2 cups (1 pint) whipping cream, divided
1 teaspoon vanilla extract
1 cup (6 ounces) miniature semi-sweet chocolate chips, divided
    Grated semi-sweet chocolate and/or strawberries (optional)

1. In small mixing bowl, dissolve coffee crystals in water; set aside
1 tablespoon coffee mixture. Brush remaining coffee mixture on cut
sides of ladyfingers; set aside.

2. In large mixing bowl, gradually beat ¾ cup Eagle Brand and mascarpone.
Add 1¼ cups whipping cream, vanilla and reserved 1 tablespoon coffee
mixture; beat until soft peaks form. Fold in half the chips.

3. In heavy saucepan over low heat, melt remaining chips with remaining
Eagle Brand.

4. Using 8 tall dessert glasses or parfait glasses, layer mascarpone mixture,
chocolate mixture and ladyfinger pieces, beginning and ending with
mascarpone mixture. Cover and chill at least 4 hours.

5. In medium mixing bowl, beat remaining ¾ cup whipping cream until soft
peaks form. To serve, spoon whipped cream over dessert. Garnish as desired.
Store covered in refrigerator.

Tiramisu

Rustic Honey Polenta Cake

Makes 12 servings

2½ cups all-purpose flour
1 cup yellow cornmeal
2 tablespoons baking powder
1 teaspoon salt
1 cup (2 sticks) butter or margarine, melted
1¾ cups milk
¾ cup honey
2 eggs, slightly beaten
Honey-Orange Syrup (recipe follows)
Sweetened whipped cream and orange segments for garnish (optional)

In large bowl, combine flour, cornmeal, baking powder and salt; mix well. In small bowl, combine melted butter, milk, honey and eggs; mix well. Stir into flour mixture, mixing until just blended. Pour into lightly greased 13×9-inch baking pan.

Bake at 325°F for 25 to 30 minutes or until toothpick comes out clean. Meanwhile, prepare Honey-Orange Syrup. When cake is done, remove from oven to wire rack. Pour hot syrup evenly over top of cake, spreading if necessary to cover entire surface. Cool completely. Garnish with dollop of whipped cream and orange segments, if desired.

Honey-Orange Syrup: In small saucepan, whisk together ½ cup honey, 3 tablespoons orange juice concentrate and 1 tablespoon freshly grated orange peel. Heat over medium-high heat until mixture begins to boil. Remove from heat; keep warm.

Favorite recipe from **National Honey Board**

BelGioioso® Gorgonzola Spread

Makes 8 servings

2 cups BELGIOIOSO® Mascarpone
½ cup BELGIOIOSO® Gorgonzola
2 tablespoons chopped fresh basil
½ cup chopped walnuts
   Sliced apples and pears

In small bowl, combine BelGioioso Mascarpone, BelGioioso Gorgonzola and basil. Mix to blend well. Transfer mixture to serving bowl; cover and refrigerate 2 hours. Before serving, sprinkle with walnuts and arrange sliced apples and pears around bowl.

Tip: This spread can also be served with fresh vegetables, crackers, Melba toast or bread.

Chocolate-Amaretto Ice

Makes 4 servings

¾ cup sugar
½ cup HERSHEY¡S Cocoa
2 cups (1 pint) light cream or half-and-half
2 tablespoons Amaretto (almond-flavored liqueur)
   Sliced almonds (optional)

1. Stir together sugar and cocoa in small saucepan; gradually stir in light cream. Cook over low heat, stirring constantly, until sugar dissolves and mixture is smooth and hot. Do not boil.

2. Remove from heat; stir in liqueur. Pour into 8-inch square pan. Cover; freeze until firm, stirring several times before mixture freezes. Scoop into dessert dishes. Serve frozen. Garnish with sliced almonds, if desired.

Fig and Hazelnut Cake

Makes 12 to 16 servings

¾ cup hazelnuts (about 4 ounces), skins removed and coarsely chopped
¾ cup whole dried figs (about 4 ounces), coarsely chopped
⅔ cup slivered blanched almonds (about 3 ounces), coarsely chopped
3 ounces semisweet chocolate, finely chopped
⅓ cup diced candied orange peel
⅓ cup diced candied lemon peel
3 eggs
½ cup sugar
1¼ cups all-purpose flour
1¾ teaspoons baking powder
¾ teaspoon salt

1. Preheat oven to 300°F. Grease 8×4-inch loaf pan. Combine hazelnuts, figs, almonds, chocolate and candied orange and lemon peels in medium bowl; mix well.

2. Beat eggs and sugar in large bowl with electric mixer at high speed at least 5 minutes or until mixture is pale yellow and thick and fluffy. Gently fold nut mixture into egg mixture.

3. Combine flour, baking powder and salt in small bowl. Sift ½ of flour mixture over nut-egg mixture and gently fold in; repeat with remaining flour mixture.

4. Spread batter evenly into prepared pan. Bake 60 to 70 minutes or until top is deep golden brown and firm to the touch. Cool in pan on wire rack 5 minutes. Remove loaf from pan; cool completely on wire rack (at least 4 hours).

Fig and Hazelnut Cake

Quick Tiramisu

Makes 6 to 8 servings

1 package (18 ounces) NESTLÉ® TOLL HOUSE® Refrigerated Sugar Cookie
    Bar Dough
1 package (8 ounces) ⅓ less fat cream cheese
½ cup granulated sugar
¾ teaspoon TASTER'S CHOICE® 100% Pure Instant Coffee dissolved in ¾ cup
    cold water, *divided*
1 container (8 ounces) frozen nondairy whipped topping, thawed
1 tablespoon NESTLÉ® TOLL HOUSE® Baking Cocoa

PREHEAT oven to 325°F.

DIVIDE cookie dough into 20 pieces. Shape into 2½×1-inch oblong shapes.
Place on ungreased baking sheets.

BAKE for 10 to 12 minutes or until light golden brown around edges. Cool
on baking sheets for 1 minute; remove to wire racks to cool completely.

BEAT cream cheese and sugar in large mixer bowl until smooth. Beat
in ¼ cup Taster's Choice. Fold in whipped topping. Layer 6 cookies in
8-inch-square baking dish. Sprinkle each cookie with *1 teaspoon* Taster's
Choice. Spread *one-third* cream cheese mixture over cookies. Repeat layers
2 more times with *12* cookies, *remaining* coffee and *remaining* cream cheese
mixture. Cover; refrigerate for 2 to 3 hours. Crumble *remaining* cookies
over top. Sift cocoa over cookies. Cut into squares.

Tip: Traditional tiramisu recipes call for sponge cake
or ladyfingers layered with mascarpone (rich
Italian cream cheese) and grated chocolate.
Modern versions of the recipe offer new twists
on the original and they can be just as delicious!

Acknowledgments

*The publisher would like to thank the companies and organizations
listed below for the use of their recipes and photographs
in this publication.*

Barilla America, Inc.

BelGioioso® Cheese, Inc.

Bob Evans®

California Olive Industry

Cucina Classica Italiana, Inc.

Del Monte Corporation

Dole Food Company, Inc.

Eagle Brand® Sweetened Condensed Milk

Filippo Berio® Olive Oil

The Golden Grain Company®

Hershey Foods Corporation

Hillshire Farm®

Holland House® is a registered trademark of Mott's, LLP

The Kingsford Products Company

McIlhenny Company (TABASCO® brand Pepper Sauce)

Mrs. Dash®

National Honey Board

National Pork Board

Nestlé USA

Perdue Farms Incorporated.

Reckitt Benckiser Inc.

Sargento® Foods Inc.

Sonoma® Dried Tomatoes

Unilever Bestfoods North America

VOLUME MEASUREMENTS (dry)

$1/8$ teaspoon = 0.5 mL
$1/4$ teaspoon = 1 mL
$1/2$ teaspoon = 2 mL
$3/4$ teaspoon = 4 mL
1 teaspoon = 5 mL
1 tablespoon = 15 mL
2 tablespoons = 30 mL
$1/4$ cup = 60 mL
$1/3$ cup = 75 mL
$1/2$ cup = 125 mL
$2/3$ cup = 150 mL
$3/4$ cup = 175 mL
1 cup = 250 mL
2 cups = 1 pint = 500 mL
3 cups = 750 mL
4 cups = 1 quart = 1 L

VOLUME MEASUREMENTS (fluid)

1 fluid ounce (2 tablespoons) = 30 mL
4 fluid ounces ($1/2$ cup) = 125 mL
8 fluid ounces (1 cup) = 250 mL
12 fluid ounces ($1 1/2$ cups) = 375 mL
16 fluid ounces (2 cups) = 500 mL

WEIGHTS (mass)

$1/2$ ounce = 15 g
1 ounce = 30 g
3 ounces = 90 g
4 ounces = 120 g
8 ounces = 225 g
10 ounces = 285 g
12 ounces = 360 g
16 ounces = 1 pound = 450 g

DIMENSIONS

$1/16$ inch = 2 mm
$1/8$ inch = 3 mm
$1/4$ inch = 6 mm
$1/2$ inch = 1.5 cm
$3/4$ inch = 2 cm
1 inch = 2.5 cm

OVEN TEMPERATURES

250°F = 120°C
275°F = 140°C
300°F = 150°C
325°F = 160°C
350°F = 180°C
375°F = 190°C
400°F = 200°C
425°F = 220°C
450°F = 230°C

BAKING PAN SIZES

Utensil	Size in Inches/Quarts	Metric Volume	Size in Centimeters
Baking or	$8 \times 8 \times 2$	2 L	$20 \times 20 \times 5$
Cake Pan	$9 \times 9 \times 2$	2.5 L	$23 \times 23 \times 5$
(square or	$12 \times 8 \times 2$	3 L	$30 \times 20 \times 5$
rectangular)	$13 \times 9 \times 2$	3.5 L	$33 \times 23 \times 5$
Loaf Pan	$8 \times 4 \times 3$	1.5 L	$20 \times 10 \times 7$
	$9 \times 5 \times 3$	2 L	$23 \times 13 \times 7$
Round Layer	$8 \times 1 1/2$	1.2 L	20×4
Cake Pan	$9 \times 1 1/2$	1.5 L	23×4
Pie Plate	$8 \times 1 1/4$	750 mL	20×3
	$9 \times 1 1/4$	1 L	23×3
Baking Dish	1 quart	1 L	—
or Casserole	$1 1/2$ quart	1.5 L	—
	2 quart	2 L	—